T H

H I S

E Y E S

O N L Y

A Collection of Poems From 1966–1980 by Leigh Clay

M A R L E N E   C L A Y

Tellwell Talent
www.tellwell.ca

ISBN
978-0-2288-5792-1 (Paperback)

FOREWORD

This book of poems is written by my late husband Leigh Everett James Clay, and, through his eyes, reflects how he discovered the beauty in nature as he grew up and the cathartic way he expressed his emotions about life and love.

Leigh transcribed the many years of poetry he wrote into two small hard bound books and gave one to me on our first Christmas together in 1980 with the following inscription.

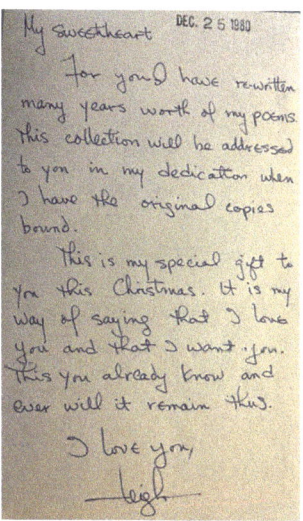

Publishing these poems is a legacy to a man with immense creative ability that I wanted to share with the world. The descriptive way he writes will leave the reader with vivid images in their mind's eye.

Leigh Clay, Lake Louise,
Alberta, circa 1982

September 1983

Marlene Clay

If nothing ever changed,
there would be no such
things as butterflies.

Wendy Mass

BUTTERFLY   JUNE 1966

How in the hell
can you just sit there
laughing,
when somewhere
a butterfly just died.

THREE

A broken toy
is what we have now
crushed like a dream.

Making love hurts
when water breaks stones
into pebbles.

Sun rises quickly
without fear of night
but dread of clouds.

STILL WHILE WALKING

A quiet walk
along the waterfront
at morning light
can be a revelation
of mist and still water
if the stillness
is only broken
by the loon.

A POEM FOR WHOMEVER
INVENTED INTELLIGENCE QUOTAS

I know some people
who spit on the floor
and say that they are testing
for echoes
in the hallway.

I also know some others
who would urinate on the floor
in the washroom
in order to make a comparison
between echoes and water rushing.

HOW YOU FEEL

Speak.

Cast away all of those ideas
of what I might have been
before your sun
touched my eyes.

Hold me forever
so that we won't grow so tall
that our friends
shall not be able to see us.

Hold me forever.
Bite your tongue
each time
that your mind lies
and says that we are not
like the strongest storm
that ever roared
through these mountains.

BEING AWARE OF NIGHT WALKING

Clean-shaven and bold
I conquer the streets
after dark.

Something in the scent
of the air
is somehow awakening
the darkness in me,
where only the streetlights
can color the depth
of my night power
within the reflection
of rain on the roadway.

OLD SILHOUETTES

When old memories
best our attempts to flee
from our own madness,
we sit around asking questions
of ourselves,
never thinking of how slow
of a death
the truth can become.

We love each other now
but all old silhouettes fade
into morning light.

AGAIN ANOTHER SPRING

I sit here
in front of the TV
with the cat playing
my socks into a nightmare,
and I can see why
your body
has the same curves
as the cherry tree
in spring.

BUBBLES

Have you ever noticed
the bubbles
that follow the surf
back
into the womb,
as though afraid
of earthly sunlight
and the scurry of the crab.

WE WHO BECOME SHADOWS

I touch your face,
your lips,
I feel your breath
upon my fingers.

When we succumb to the night,
I feel the moistness
of your anticipation of me
and we become the softest corner
of the night's shadows.

ROCKIES

Because
the rain caresses the mountains
in summer,
our love will not spite the rain
for its boldness.

When winter buries
our comfort
beneath tons of ice and snow
our hearts will still melt
before the fire.

Because the Rockies
are cast of my stone,
not even hellwind
will force us from them.

RETURN

When I left the farm
it was as though
I had been careless
with my goodbyes.

I want to come back
to you of meadows green,
of reeds at the pond's-side
and golden, swaying oats
under the breath
of the wind,
because I am quite simply
choking
on this outer filth.

WORDS

My love,
I write for you
words
as simple and slender
as wild grasses
that sway windblown
on the crest
of the bluff.

ON LOVING

When the evening side
of our loving
has melted into night,
we come together
where the grass is sweet
and the air finds us
free from shame and hesitation.

PART OF A WHOLE

If you ever want to see
gentility
as a part of a more supreme
power,
watch the ice crystal
tumble safely over a rock
in a mountain stream
nourished by glacial swell.

FIRESIDE

Meet me at the fireside
and court me through
the night.

Watch the sparks
hurry from the logs
when I melt your lips
with my tropical warmth.

Meet me at the fireside
and court me
like a furious statement,
the way the gorge
courts the fool
high above
on a too narrow rock ledge.

CAUGHT AT THE HEADLAND

Whilst waiting for the breakers
to calm at this headland,
we sat huddled
for shelter
beneath this up-turned canoe,
listening to the roar of the wind
in the rocks
and wondering how many other forts
were caught here,
warmed by dozens
of long-dead campfires.

LAKESHORE DARKNESS

The heat of your skin,
and of your hand
playing soft tides in my hair
set the kindling to flame
where your hand touched me.

We were so easy
upon each other
that our moving scarcely disturbed
a blade of grass
nor did we trouble the sand
beneath us.

WEATHER CHANGING

Walking through the park
I notice the lovers
with their arms wound
around each other
like ivy on telephone poles.

The swans in the pond
rub the algae
from each other's necks
then thrust their heads again
beneath the murky water
to stir up the refuse
left by a better day.

Dogs chase tossed balls
and children chase each other
as rainclouds loom.

RIVERGRASS

When my winds
whisper through the fields
and bend your hair
like reeds,
we will feel our bodies
bending together
in time to the wind's ripples
in the rivergrass.

MORE THAN JUST MY TOUCH

You wanted a poem
from me,
but what you needed
was a heart that was not pretentious
and full of shadows,
like the lonely nights
that fitted in not with loving
nor the grace of the wind,
but rather with elusive fantasies
and thoughts of me
which really upset your mind.

GRADUATIONS

When I took your hand
and felt how warm it was
I thought of warmth,
and when I looked
into your eyes
I saw the fire within
and I thought of love,
but when our lips
touched,
I knew...

DON'T LET GO

If you let the sun disappear,
your lovely skin will pale
and you'll fade away
with the leaves
beneath the tree
that sheltered you,
and the arms
that pressed around you
will fade away too.

ORCHARD

Heavy with child
the lady looked from her bedroom
window
into the trees beyond.

After the child was born
she walked it within the mighty green,
because the sparrow nested there
and apples fell from boughs
in fall's whisperings.

BENEATH THE CASCADE

Each time
that you accept my heat
with a moan,
let the cascades
of your waterfall
roar
down your slopes.

AFTER THE FIRE BURNS DOWN

When the fire burns down
and the wind
breaks into a caress,
will you walk with me
on this shoreline
and marvel at the moonlight
on the rocks
and cresting waves.

DRAINING

When those progress-minded
and so-called modern
farmers
cut furrows in their fields
to drain the marshes
and duck-ponds
to create more flesh
for planting,
it is as suddenly paleing
as watching the blood rush
from a newly slit wrist.

COVERINGS

Only the trees
can shed their leaves
the way
that I wish to blanket you
with my love.

MALIGNE CANYON EVENING

When I look upon these pages
and my eyes begin to wander
from lack of sleep
to your stream-shaped curves,
I often wish
that I was the water
which caresses you constantly
like a polished pebble
so that I may find slumber,
like slow-moving water
on round stones.

COOL OF THE EVENING

When I reach out for you
and you are eager for my touch,
you will find
that the waves
against my familiar rocks
will wrap themselves around you
like blankets
whenever you call.

SOMETIMES TWISTING

Sometimes our love
is like a broken branch–
still hanging on
by a few live fibers,
bending and twisting
helplessly
within the narrow laugh
of the wind.

WHEN WE COME TOGETHER

I could never tire of your moving
because your scent
washes over me
like the waves
of a valley lake
and the tracks of snowshoes
printed on the snow.

ISLAND FIRE

Leaves
fall only for a moment
before the snow,
and we think
that the island is dying
before the final glow.

The sky has a solemn answer
for the grey
where the horizon swells,
but our silence is known
only to us,
because our hearts rage
like that island fire.

OATFIELD

At night
when the moon hung
like blue-white laughter
over the oats,
I would run through the field
and turn around at the end
to look at the black furrow
that I had aroused,
only to see the wind
smooth over again
the rippling hair
of the moon's brazen child.

JUST AWAKENING

Here in the morning
is blessed silence,
save for the rain
past the eaves
and your breath
on my cheek.

SNOWSTORM

I am sure
that everyone has something to say
about this grey, bleak attitude
of nature.

It is a solemn power
that makes us shiver
beneath our bedclothes,
yet it can kindle our hearts
to flame
during the right light.

SUCH A SAD SPARK

When we spoke
of the fences between us,
a lot of things
that you said by the water
finally produced flames
when I sat on the cliff rocks
and watched a dam being built
further upstream.

PROMISE

You needed a verse
to take away the life
from your unsureness,
and I promised my best effort
with a winter's evening
guarantee.

When I reached out
and touched you
I did my best to keep my word
by folding you into my night
of beloved wind,
of surrendering moon
and wine ---
chilled just so.

NIGHT LIKE THE SEA

When the darkness
melts in on the poplars
it fills in the evening
like water around rocks.

With a soft whisper
through moonlit branches,
breezes ebb and flow
like waves on the strand
when this evening sea
stretches into the forest
like seaweed in a current.

FIREWIND WITHIN

When beneath this moon
the sagebrush
filled your nostrils with night
you told me that you'd never leave
this partial desert,
this rain-starved wasteland,
because your heart burned
beneath the rage
and limitless firewind
of such loving.

BEFORE AN OPEN WINDOW

Loosen up completely
beneath the soft tread
of my fingers.

You wanted to know
the sound of wind
through pines
where the moonlight slept,
so accept
the infinite pull of the tide
and the touch of my hands.

RIVER SHINING

When I sit here in the dark
with the night tuned down
I can hear the river
rushing
outside my window,
and I dream of being polished
by our loves
like the pebbles within the currents.

PARTY

When everyone is laying around
passed out on the floor
or throwing up in the bathroom,
I can feel well about the evening
because I drank my wine
outside.

FIRE

The journey of our love
is an inverted abyss
where the limit
is the ne'er ending stars,
and my love is tame enough
yet fire wild
like my mouth
upon your breast.

THIRTY-SECOND STREET CHRISTMAS

A drunken old vagrant
stumbled out of an alley
and fell in the snow
at my feet.

I heard the bone go
in his arm
but I doubt that he felt it.
I tried to help him
to his feet
but he shrugged me off,
cursing and mumbling
at a broken, half smoked cigarette
that he was trying to light
with a wet match.

EARLY

I can remember
when the rising sun
found me awake
by hours
ahead of the rooster.

I was always first
to see the wild turkeys
grubbing in the brush
and the first autumn leaves
turning over in the morning
within a fresh, new wind.

NIGHT WIND

When the darkness
allows me to touch your lips
and my hands to roam
wild
and nightswept,
you will soon feel
that touching can be as honest
as loving into morning light.

SOME SAY THAT THE CITY IS A MEADOW

Some say
that the city
is as comforting
as meadows under the sun,
but when it's time
for me to walk through it
I find that there are
snakes in the grass
and too damn many stones
hiding the weasels.

ABOVE THE OUTWASH

Slim waterfalls
tumble down this mountainside
like wisps of your golden hair
melting over your face
when sleep comes.

SWAYING

When you show me
how strong
your laugh can be
I will show you cattails
that bloom only
in fall
when strong winds bend things
beyond your breath.

CERTAIN PEOPLE

Some people I know
are like a toilet;
they must be flushed
and disinfected frequently
to keep them clean
and free from clogging.

ALONE ON THE SHORELINE

How slowly my nights
pass
when your boats
have all put
to sea.

RISING

Can you let me touch you
the way the meadow flower
brushes
against the sky
on its way sunward
from the grass
around its waist.

WIND DANCE

When the music played
I watched you dance
and whirl yourself
into wind
for me.

WITH THE THOUGHT

Touch me with the thought
that you felt
when it rained,
and I will touch you
with the thought
that I remembered
after the storm.

JUST BEFORE DOCKING

When you left me alone with my love
in the wind and the salt-spray
on the deck of the ferry,
I knew then that your soul
and your next love
would become
like the dead and tide-borne
seaweed
that brushes even now
against the hull
of this huge boat.

MORNING'S FIRST BIRDSONG

Maybe by the time
that the first yellow light
of morning
creeps over the windowsill,
we will have found
an answer for the bird
that sings his way
into our awakening.

FLIGHT AWAY

I missed you
when I left.

Your shoulders
were warm and soft
beneath my hands
and I now think of the miles
between us
as being quick breaths
in the darkness.

PASSAGES

When the morning mist
settles in
at the foot of the mountain
and the peaks are soon lost
to our eyes,
do we need to worry
for those golden leaves
that rock back and forth
wind-moved on their stems
before they assign bare limbs
to the autumn skyline.

FIVE

Can you love me
as hard
as the icicle forms.

When you touch me
I wear your lips
like wind in the leaves.

I dream of you
when nights become black
before the mornings.

When the barrow breaks
I am the pin
that sets your wooden wheel.

Bubbles are all
that are left
of our love.

US TOGETHER

I want you to be
moist upon me
as we stream
back and forth
in the surge
of our loving,
for there are no pebbles
in the current
of our melding
to slow us.

READING THROUGH

Open any novel
to the very last page
and you can see why
there are heroes
and why there are lovers
that aren't much different
in their eagerness
for the grave.

REMEMBERING THE MARSH

It is really quite late
considering the love
that I have missed
of your arms
when the woodpecker awakens me
beside my row of beer bottles
at dawn.

MOUNTAIN MORNING

In the morning
when you awaken by the stream,
kick out all of the cobwebs
and wash your face
in water that is cold enough
to bring you running back
to me.

WHEN YOU TEASE ME

'Don't tease the cat',
grandpa said.
'It's a creature of the night
and it can scratch
viciously'.

DEDICATION

The years crumble stone walls
into sorry pebbles
where the seasons wear their edges
into dull blades
of remaining stone.

Though we have not as yet
loved in the grass,
please don't crumble me
or try to wear me down
because we become older
and burdened.

We must still have our chance,
all else aside,
and we'll tie ourselves together
like the mortar holding together
the remnants of these aged stones.

Sugar Lake, British Columbia, 1974

OFFERING

As I lay here at night
listening to the blues
on the radio
I think of the talks we had
at the lakeshore cabin
when the chill of the wind
drove you inside
and left me full of words.

If I could spill myself out
on the waves
I could flood the world
a hundred times over
until the birds came to me
for a sign.

ROCKY MOUNTAIN MORNING

A torrent of white water
tumbles downward
from ledge to rocky ledge.

It's passage-bed drops away
into the mist-clouded coldness
about the valley
as though it was a stone stairway
hewn into the living rock.

It reaches the lakes
and mirelands below
where moose graze at leisure
amongst the reeds
and early morning dampness
before the sun burns
through
the clustered fog blanket.

STEALING LOVE

Wasted nights are frequent.

We unlock our love
like a thief
who arrives only after
the building has been shut
to friends.

FLOW

I'm thinking of you
so far away
that I can hardly wait
for the water in my streams
to touch you at the ocean.

PASSING THROUGH WILLIAMS LAKE

I've been half awake
and half asleep
on this night-ridden Greyhound
for nearly nine hours now.

The bus jerks
each time the driver changes gears
and I can't remember the last time
that I felt so fine
as when your head
was nestled against my chest.

JOURNEY

Rocks tumble down
with the torrents
from broken mountains above,
and they become smooth
like love
near the bottom.

SOFTLY FROZEN

When our lips touch
our breaths whisper
as snow blowing
across the glacier.

RUMORS

Upstairs
I can hear my roommate
pounding his urgency into his lover
upon a mattress
which is not much better
than mine.
I would rather
that our love be heard
by the meadow
where flowers bend
to the wind,
than by ears which bend and flex
to rumor.

BEFORE THE ALBERTA RAIN

Before the arrival of the rain,
the poplars
would have an hour's grace
to turn their leaves around
in the breeze
and line the forest with silver
before the blackness of thunder clouds
covered
even the moss
on the north side of the pines
beneath a shuddering, navy blanket.

METAMORPHOSIS

Like a butterfly
we grow in phases
of color and transparency.

Each time that my lips touch yours
and our flesh welds itself
together,
this metamorphosis expands
to include all parts of us
and not merely sunsets.

DRIVEN WIND

Though I am promised
to someone else,
you have become
my precious wind
and have forced yourself
into me.

CONFINES

Before going to bed
I thought of you
being so many miles away
and sea-swept,
and I wondered how it would be
if you were here
loving me
and sleeping with me
on this narrow green mattress
which is almost like grass.

WHEN YOU GO AWAY

Each time
that I spend the night alone
without you
the stars seem to go out
like snuffed candles
where only the smoke of darkness
rises
and scents the air.

SPEAK IN RIDDLES

Think of things
which lend themselves
to thoughts.

Speak of times
of which justice is done
with words,
but when speaking of me
speak quietly in riddles
of moon,
of wind and waves.

Leigh Clay, Central Alberta, circa 1959

A CHILD DOES NOT
THINK OF HORIZONS

While I was only
a child
I never dreamt of you
because the wind
through the poplars
mentioned no names.

Knowing of things
is a result of growing,
but I can't feel the new limbs
because I don't hear
the poplars whispering to me
their secrets
as they did
when my childhood eyes
did not set horizons
beyond wild rose bushes.

Marlene Clay

WATERFALL

The mountain's downward breath
tumbles and froths
over smoothened rocks
and bark-stripped logs
before it disappears below.

RUNNING EACH NIGHT

I don't want to be a man
running
to your loving each night.
I need it there
where I can easily find it
beneath our candles.

FASTEST JOURNEY THROUGH

Down on mainstreet
where the dust swirls
and papers twist
in the wind,
I calculate how long
it will take
for me to run
from here to the next block,
to the next block,
to the next…

FITTING IN

Learning to make love to you
is like a tree
getting used to its new leaves
after a strenuous winter
when the only thing
that moved with vigor
was wind-driven snow.

LAST TIDE

When I see your photos
strung across your wall,
like bubbles in the surf,
I try to imagine how long
it will take
before we begin to lie
to one another
about the hour of the last
tide.

LIMITS

If you've never made love
where the scent of wild roses
is so strong
that you are overcome
with evening,
you've never slept
with anyone
beyond your limited window.

BLOWING

Though I am quick
to feel the loving touch
I am quicker to feel
the wind
after it
passes.

FIVE

Yesterday faded slowly
into today
new clouds form.

Where the sun once was
lies the night
where darkness blackens leaves.

Our love
can endure the snow
until it melts.

When the evening
touches your lips
touch me with yours.

Close your eyes
my fingers are agile
and wear my love.

SPARE THIS LANDSCAPE

You speak of the fun
that you have
churning up the turf
with your dirt bike.
Even though I love you
I don't want your touch
to grind up my strawberries.

MAKING LOVE

Each time
when the moment is ripe
and we lay twisted together
exploding like bombs
through each other's skin,
I reach out to catch that wind
that brushes us with love
only to feel it
slip through my fingers
and brush us again.

MOVEMENTS

Loving you
can sometimes be as swift
as the wind
through the rivergrass
and yet as slow
as an autumn leaf
dropping hesitantly
to a thin stream
below the touch.

DUSTSTORM

When the wind
is like a spear
through your hair
and you can't see the roadway
for dust,
let the bareness of your feet
touch the stones.

Precede your horse afoot
through the blowing leaves.

WHEN WAVES FORM

When the darkness
leaves the lake
and the moon floods
the ripples
in the water,
let the sand form
in front of the waves.

AFTER DINING IN EDMONTON

When the moistness of you
touches home beneath my belly
I don't think of our flesh as much
as I do of the union
of summer and fall
and of the evening wine
of our extended meal.

TONING DOWN

Often
love must be a timid thing.
We tire
of the surging beast;
it tires us out
chasing its breath,
trying to contain
and manipulate it.

Love must be a timid thing
for no wild beast
is gentle by choice
or loves the moon
for its gleam.

SKIING

When you sprayed me
with snow
from the slope,
I felt your wind
as being
my first winter laugh.

BETWEEN THESE SATIN SHEETS

I love you
for the way that you moan,
and I love you
for the way that your scent
drives me madly into your arms.

EARLY SUN

When you wore your lonliness
like a heavy remembrance
of a mountain stream
in mid-summer,
I promised you a leaf
which had not as yet
fallen
into autumn,
so that you would feel the approach
of the early sun.

OVER THE RIMS

In this morning-lit tent
our guitars form the sounds
of morning winds
gliding over rocks
that face
into deep valleys.

THOSE THAT MISS

When I count
the boulders
at the lakeshore,
I count, too, the waves
that fail to break
against their hardness.

IMAGE BEYOND ICE

I hope that you had
a good Christmas.
I saw snowshoe tracks
going through the poplars
to the lakeshore
where the sand lies frozen
and the grass sleeps
beneath the forced and hurried breath
of the wind.

BEFORE THE SURGE

When you moan beneath me
in the darkness,
I find the quickness of our breaths
melting into the roar
of a mountain stream
before tumbling into the grey scree
below.

ON RELIGION

Your face
is like an un-weathered stone –
too rough,
too misshapen
to recognize men
or to love
honestly.

LET HIM RECOGNIZE THE SHAPING

When the forest
becomes dark
because someone defies
the river,
do not let his heart drown
before knowing
that his mind
is forever shifting away
from the ever-carving current.

WHEN MORNING COMES IN

When the curtains
are thrust aside
and the morning sun
blisters in through the glass
onto our bed,
taste me
hot
and gentle upon you.

TODAY'S SPARROWS

When the end of day
has come
and the road winds
its dust
away into haze,
the sun makes no sound
as it falls behind
the horizon
where today's sparrows
have gone to fly.

DESERT OBSERVATION

When the sidewinder
leaves his ripples
in the sand,
he needs no recipe
for those
who cannot escape
his evening meal.

ROCKY MOUNTAIN VISTA

Only the raging
courses
of the streams
remain open
during winter's freeze-up,
where pine and spruce
check their ice-bound, stony banks.

Looming, grey
monoliths
of mountain peaks
glare silently and aristocratically
over the eternal green,
snow-laden grin
of the lower valleys
whilst a black storm builds
behind their ice-rock
pates.

LOVE ON THE BLUFF

When the lake waves
crush the rocks together,
meet me on the bluff
where we will
show the night how to fold
in upon itself.

MOTIONS

Isn't the water
like a bed
where promises are acted upon
before morning walks
in spring orchards
and on sun-swelled lakeshores.

ALBERTA WINDSTORM

Back on the farm
we would have windstorms,
great, foreboding black ogres
that would loom up
over time-shrunken foothills
and darken the air.

Before the great moment
the air would move about
like a hesitant child
unsure of his step.

Then,
summoning all of its courage,
the wind would hurl its abuse
through distant trees
and come roaring forward,
churning up clouds of black dust
and filling its belly with straw.

In the face of its anger,
it tore branches from the poplars
and flung them against the walls
of the farmhouse
and passing overhead,
groaning and howling
like a turbine that had gone mad.

Marlene Clay

TWO

Dizziness
like an unfolding heart
opening up to love.

Leaves in autumn
turn yellow, red and brown
fall softly to the ground.

AMONG THE REEDS

How warm
the sand is
after a day of being touched
by the sun.

How brightly
your eyes gleam
upon finding me
alone
among swaying afternoon reeds.

SHANDRA

Once I was here,
but not long enough to forget.
I need to forget.

Chasing after grey
and worrying over mysteries
that chastised us
for not loving in the dark,
never left us much comfort
behind tall windows.

We wanted the whole world
to see us,
to see how good we were
for each other,
but all the world ever gave us
were echoes and marks in the dust...
all empty
like footprints in the sand.

QUEST FOR THE NEXT STEP

An old diagnosis of love
spoke of stars,
of holding hands
and of waiting eagerly
behind the fence
at the airport.

Now it speaks only
of whom is responsible
for which half
of the relationship,
and of whom puts out
the trash
on Friday.

UNFOLD

Before the sun
has a chance to burst,
welcome me like a breeze
to your un-opened
petals.

VISIONS BEFORE THE FOREST

Some of us cease
to eagerly await daylight
because we've forgotten
our secret visions.

We shut down our attention
and die from exposure
beneath the ice of those daily things
which become commonplace,
because rituals seem too silly
to be enjoyably legitimate.

We are colorful
under the dead mat of autumn leaves
but not poignant
like the leaves which haven't fallen.

We commit ourselves
to the grave
when we whisper about rules,
about the morals and duties,
but the forest does not care
what we say to our lovers
in abandonment.

WOMAN TRAIN

As I lay here at night
listening to the stillness,
a train shivers by
and hammers its presence
into the rails,
jarring the quietude
and shattering the contemplation
of the darkness
and cricket orchestra
with its short-lived chatter.

Finally
the caboose nears and passes,
shrinking
as it creaks away into the black,
with its yellow light
grinning through square patches
of half-pulled windowshades.

You are that train
young woman.
I see only a little light
here and there – in patches,
and always on the same side
of the truth,
as it too
shrinks into the darkness.

ISLAND

I am the waves
which raise up your shore
beneath the momentary pull
of the moon.

I am the water-forced breath
which washes each of your stones
with my tide-driven heart.

RECONSIDER

Whom is it
that benefits most by the firefly
when the lights outside
and those inside
go off in tune with the shutters.

Groping in this ink
it is us, my fatal compromise.
It is us
who pour ourselves out in bed
like warm bourbon from a bottle.

BEFORE

Before the moon
threaded the ripples
in the water with light,
your heart was on fire
with an image.

Now that the water
has passed beneath the bridge
and the sailboats have gone home,
the flame cringes
in your only candle.

CHANGE OF SCENE

Curtains lean over windows
like eyelids hang over your eyes.
I can always see
the hint of a shadow
under there,
a veil which diffuses out
too much light
for you to see
how real we could become.

Perhaps we could try it on
in the dark
where light is unimportant
and distantly melancholy.

ABOVE THE BREAKERS

While the sun
sprays the bluff
with yellow,
leave your sandwashed shellfish
and heaving breakers
to come to the cliffs
where I wait
above the swell and thunder.

ARGUMENT

With our hands
we brush aside
the moon's wide filament
on the river
and our teeth tell us
how cold the night.

Our love is in the distance
where baying wolves plead hunger,
but instead of reaching for it
by this moonlight,
we sit here and grind axes.

ELIMINATION

This immediate world
of waiting, and waiting longer
amongst angry faces
and dead pets, lies and heat...
has no bearing;
has no bearing on the immediate state
of one's soul,
because the duties and manners
of time and religion
tear the heart out first.

BEAT

If I could but decipher
the rhythm of the wind
through the reeds,
through the pines above
yellow, flowing grasses,
I could hear the beat
of your heart
through your sweater.

AWAITING AUTUMN

Once upon this wooded hill
my eyes met the valley below
searching out some vivid spray
of autumn leaves,
but the sky closed in
all around
and welded me inside
its blue belly.

I probe for that chill
of night, and that smoke
that renders the season apparent,
but the hot, dusty veil of summer
still floats weightlessly
on every horizon.

TO A STEP-FATHER

Each time
that I called out for your love,
all that I ever saw
was the velvet blue smoke
from the spinning tires
of that old, battered Chevrolet..

a surging projectile
trying to get away.

WAVES

Words of love
are always much sweeter
when put to the music
of waves
beneath the only moon.

OVERLAND VIEW

Looking out
over this vast and crumbled landscape,
I can easily imagine
how many years
it must have taken
to lay down and die like this.
Yet
there is so much
of it left,
so much to go on weathering
and bragging of time
in wrinkled old skin.

AMY'S SMILE

For some time now
you've been losing the color
from your smile.

Now
I can read only
the black and white technicalities.

The gestures
which used to curve your face
have fallen slack
and incomplete.

Where are the roses –
where are the jungle flowers,
Amy?

BEFORE THE TIDE

When the candle
shudders in the breeze,
touch me
before the ocean's tide
reaches my castles.

CHILD

The man said
that young ducklings grow up
and fly away.

The child ran
and hid
under her father's wing.

BRICK BY BRICK

When I was building
my towers of wisdom
you spoke only of the lovers you'd had,
the stableman in Victoria,
the psychology major at U.B.C.,
the others.

Yet,
when your nakedness touches me
I can feel you
as tense
as a dry, bending willow.

MOVINGS

I'm going to show
the mist
where to go
to cover you
with morning.

Beaver River, British Columbia

AND WHAT OF ME

Behind that leafless cluster,
those trees on the ridge,
lie the legends of the deer
and of those who strayed there.

Now those willows sleep
in winter's cold mystery,
although not so mysterious to us,
eh, Butterfly?

Can you see the toboggans,
the friends and lovers
blazing like happy bullets
down the slope,
and do you remember
the silence
that followed them.

ALBERTA FARMHOUSE

Spring rains drip down from the eaves
around this old farmhouse.
Moss-covered shingles
weathered by the sun,
reach upward like bent teeth.
Old poplar trees dismiss their leaves
onto the pathway
that leads to a battered screen door
hanging on one hinge.
Winter snows take refuge
in the chinks between the logs
where the mortar and moss
has long since fallen
away.

ELLISON BEACH

When the flame
soars above the candle,
my lips will melt yours
beneath the moon
on this day-warmed
boulder
at the head
of the waves.

OBSERVATION

I went walking
through an old, forgotten graveyard;
the tombstones were toppled down
and scattered in the grass
like the toys of forgetful children.

ATTACHMENTS

Sitting
without even a drink
in this Prince Rupert
hotel room,
watching the rain
fall incessantly outside,
is like washing the laundry
into oblivion.

SUE HAREUTHER

I lay here confused
in a state of dreams and fantasies,
looking to mend
the broken bowl
of happiness,
but when I find the pieces
I probably won't know where to start
to assemble them
into one perfect moment
with you.

BEHIND MEADOW CURTAINS

The indentation
that we made
in the grass
was our only reminder
of how carefully
and gently
the curtains wavered,
tousled by the breeze.

YOUR ANGEL HAS HORNS

I have held your hand
when you were cold.
I have touched your lips
when I was bold.
I have gained your love
through all the thorns
but now I find
that your angel has horns.

OCEANGRASS

When shadows move
with this candlelight
I think of us
moving
and making our own
shadows
above this ocean's
seascape.

MIDDLE AGE TRAGEDY

Today
there are too many men
sitting in stairwells
or sleeping in parks,
living with the thin line of hope
shattered in their heads.
Their trembling hands
and unsure, hotel thoughts
fumble
with the buttons
of a younger girl's jeans,
while all the golden visions
of what they've dreamt of each night
for twenty-five years,
are blurred by the alcohol
and mirrored by the warm flesh
of spent, fifteen or twenty-year-old
breasts
that stare up at their hands
like wilted, drying melons
which have ripened only on one side.

TIES TO SEVER

There were all of those times
that we met secretly
until we were found out.
Then
you had the poor taste
to turn on me
and spit me out of your guilt.

Now I sit by a candlelit table
watching the light dance redly
through the cold burgundy,
trying to recall
whether or not
any of your confidences
were as solid as this chair
upon which I sit.

I know well the scent of you
because that's all you wanted to
give,
but at least
my fingers feel some reprieve
when I slam your name
into my poetry.

BEFORE SUNRISE

Before the morning
breaks
above your eyes,
I will let you know
how the night feels
before the moon.

FORCED ENTRY

Sometimes I hated the cricket
for the noise it made
in the darkness.

As I laid there in the night,
sweating and unable to sleep
in the summer's heat,
I plotted to go outside
and find it
but it eluded me
by throwing shadows
and darkness at me.

I ask myself
if you really love me
or if you just want to chirp
your way
into this already festering mind
to kill a little more of me.

ENDURING WINTER

A tree stands
cold

shivering from the frost
hiding
under the snow

its branches strained
and sagging
from burden
never saying a word
aloud

no heater
no match
to start a fire
to heat the belly of its longing
for spring.

TAILORED FOR A SONGBIRD

Early doth come the morn,
and thou, little flower,
wait for me.
Bloom with the sun,
smile with the patience
my love hath for thee.

Feel not burden nor shame
when our sun arises
through the window.
Be not far from me
whenst my touch
doth wander
with thee and only thee in mind.

AUTUMN OF THE WHEELBARROW

An old wooden wheelbarrow
lays overturned
against a poplar tree
in the yard.

A few
of the previous autumn's leaves
lay wedged
into its corners.

It will no longer support
my load
though I will ever cherish
the bumpy rides from the screen-door
to the garden,
generously rendered
by my long-dead
father.

TIMES

Love used to be
a mother's protruding belly,
but now I ain't quite so sure
if that's such a good idea.
I'm just glad
that they don't stick out so much anymore.

MEMORIES OF A ROOM

The silence in this room
creaks and groans
like heavily strained timbers
in an ancient stone building.

How can you face the past
amidst this din of silence
when it trembles in the air about you
and sweeps down into your mind
like the howling winds of winter.

POEM FOR A LOVER

I dream of you at night
my lady,
by day
I go wild in meadows.

FOR GRANNY EDL - 1972

I am sitting alone
on a cold marble stone
on which I have engraved the song
of a bluebird.

FOR GRANDMA

Little breezes bend the geraniums in the garden,
but the pain is not in the bending.
The pain lies elsewhere, hidden,
beyond reproach because it cannot be seen.
We are baffled by the breezes that bend us,
that torture our roots with the strain.
The color of that same geranium does not fade away
because of a tug here or there, nor does it falter
when some of the roots pull free.
We give up hope too easily
when that which we cannot explain
falls hard on our hearts
and molds up into thinking
'What leaf is it now
that has waylaid its home
to be apart from us?'
But when the end does come
all things pass from us in a different light.
Where once was common daylight
now shines illumination.
All those things that we forgot to do or say,
those places that we meant to frequent,
are now accessible to our pain.
But the illumination of the truth
has changed our hearts,
and when at last,
our roots can bear no more,
we come to understand the reasons
why the breezes must blow.

WALKING HOME

Long after the better memories
of town
had gone to sleep,
how did you like the night wind
tearing at your coat,
and the dust biting your eyes
whilst out walking.

Do you remember
how it tickled
when I traced the outline
of your neck
with my finger
whilst waiting for the bus.

THREE

Mushroom growing
with umbrella poised
an only roof.

Brown splinter
makes a young child cry
finger bleeding for the tree.

Summer windstorm
the trees curl earthbound
wind rushes by.

Wells Grey Provincial Park, British Columbia, 1976

FIREFLY

I go out into the black chocolate night
when the fireflies come in
like cherries banished from a crimson sunset
to light the night sky.

WELLS GREY

Oh how well
we loved each other
then,
in the early morning mist
and birdsong
of the biggest provincial park campsite
that our minds and needs
had ever turned to in abandon.

Oh how to pride and praise
those moments
when not even a mosquito
dared come nye.

Oh the way we held each other
the way the mist
held the cliffs
of Helmecken Falls

POEM

Walking in the after-rain
mist on the hill,
cool breeze through my hair.

Grass
wet and squeaking
beneath my toes.

Tulips laden with droplets,
puddles in the grass,
errant, tiny green frog
hopping to get away.

UP THE BEACH

When the surf in the distance
pounds out like drums
behind the cliffs,
come out to find me
where I stand
ahead
of the water-swelled sands,
beyond the barnacles
on the rocks
where the sun-hardened spines
of dis-membered sea urchins
lie colorful
and half-buried in the sea waste.

TIME CHORD

My lost heroes have fled
to the grasslands of home;
my fingers are lost
in the chords of this poem
of golden morning.

The scent of you lingers here
on this torn cotton sheet,
reminding me of all the times
we locked our bodies in retreat
from the chords that were played.

And when I walk alone
in the park or anywhere
along dusty streets,
the bounce of your hair
says that this present stage
is somehow all wrong.

LOOKING OUT

While sitting on the bluffs
above Kalamalka Lake,
I used to look down
on sailboats
and the train
when it thundered by,
and I would wonder
about the sunflowers
and yellow grass,
the blue of the water,
the touch of your lips
and I would wonder
again,
and again,
and again…

GUITAR

Lovely lady,
graceful shape to touch,
you make music,
you make the sounds
of love,
of fingers upon grace
like fair skin in lace.

Lovely lady
you make the sound
of water,
of a young man's daughter
laughing.

PORTLAND STREET

The truth
always has to be told
sooner or later.

I thought it wise
to inform you now
that you've died somehow.

SURGE

The wind
whips the clouds
into tears,
and rips up dust
from the earth's scalp,
but only the heart
does the wind really touch.

CHERRY-LEIGH

You remind me
of an old photo
yellowed with age –
so mellow on my mind
like a flower
I once pressed for someone
who touched me
with her eyes,
and turned with me
into the night.

ONE SUMMER IN ALBERTA

Who was that running naked
through the forest
while the afternoon sun was bleeding down
upon the river
where great rainbow trout
lay basking in sun pools.
I stand on a bridge over heaving water
and watch swarms of insects
humming, suspended,
in intermittent clusters in the shadows.
The breezes rise and fall
like the chest of a sleeping child
locked in dreams of deer playing
and squirrels yattering in the trees.
Who was that running naked
through sun-flooded meadows
where purple butterflies were diving
in and out amongst wild tiger lilies
and golden buttercups.
Who were they which filled the forest
with their laughter
until the laughter became silent,
and the only audible sounds
were splashes in the river
followed by more silence.

BLUEBIRDS

Bluebirds,
racing past the river,
singing in the willow,
sleeping in grassy pillows
in a tree.

Bluebirds,
skipping from branch to branch,
fleeing from the fang and claw
of the cat
lost in the sky's house.

Bluebirds,
in a pale crimson sunset,
flying all alone
to the land beyond the mountain's throne
to color the morning sky.

HOPE FOR YELLOW

Mud puddle lakes
just after the rain.

Long forgotten memories
drifting back,
welling up into a tear in my eye –
a tiny, shining lake
of tokens, touches and promises that crumbled,
of sun and green and wind
that only happened once
and went away.

CHILDHOOD

I watched that little boy
clutching his grandfather's hand
and I saw myself as a boy
when I chased frogs
down by the lagoon,
and caught green and yellow-lined turtles
as they sunned themselves
on rocks.

The lagoon has since been filled in
with the rubble of progress,
and the turtles have gone away,
taking their green and yellow shells
with them
into some subtle desolation
in which my plan
has not yet been recognized.

FOR YOU AND I AND THE WIND

My lady –
the way that I feel
about you now –
I could twist the wind
and hurl it
through my favourite trees.
I could make the leaves whisper.
I could make the grasses sway
in the sandy ridges
of the shore dunes.

PRESSURE POINT

Let me touch your face.
Let me end this race
between us.

Pull to me my lady,
pull away from those dead things
that still hurt you.
Fill your mind with me
my lady,
fill your mind with us.

AFTER LOVE

Your bones still need to speak
after you've delivered your love
with the appropriate muscles,
but this guilty denial could hover
like a hawk above the field mouse,
unaware,
to become a story defiled
and tedious with blood.

HAMMERING OUT A ROUTE

Those windy little conclusions
that we filtered out at the seashore
are a growing testament
as to how absurd ideas can become
when plans are made
under a too-hot sun.

We could take the rest of the day
to feel ourselves out,
but beneath what sky,
beneath what image
of promise
could we mould it
into one turbulent understanding
without being mis-quoted.

HOW IT LETS GO

When your feet are wet
with the newest dew
and there are only two of you
with the moon
and frog chorus,
show how your love blooms
like madness
when the soul lets go.

DON'T WEAR NO HURTIN' MEMORY

When the sun fell
behind its curtain of clouds,
the only words you spoke to her
were words of love,
but the only thoughts she had
were upside down.

Now the moon is shining
for no one.

She's gone away with the sea –
the splash and spray are her smile.
Her hair is the sand,
as loose as that night
in Montreal.

You don't have to wear
a hurtin' memory.
You've got to bend that needle
that sewed you to her soul.
You've got to grab that train
and flee with a smile.

THOUGHT

Oh to flow away
like the stream
and feel as courageous
as the pebbles
that are tumbled around
and worn down
beneath its water.

THOUGHT II

If I had to decipher
the codes of the wind
in the leaves,
the flower's bloom,
or why the bee stings,
would the nectar
of the wild honeysuckle
be sweet on my lips
because
I had opened my mouth
just
to taste it.

FORWARD

Name me this gentle thought,
this feeling of my flesh
upon yours.
Name for me this liberation
which burns as fire
behind me
and drives me forward
to you.

OLD JOKES

I have found
that anytime anyone
has something to see,
everyone else
is still laughing
at old jokes.

NIGHT PATROL

I'm sitting here
by this window,
watching the autumn night
and the police cruiser
turning up my street.

I am slowly getting drunk
on cold beer,
wondering
what that cop will see
and feel
at the other end
of his life.

RUNNING BY THE WAY

Sometimes
when I find you
by yourself, by the tree,
I feel as though
I have no thoughts
save for those
that let me bleed my feelings
when everyone else's blood
is running.

ANGEL GLACIER

The Angel's foot
grips the ageless, pock-marked clefts
like talons
of a long forgotten and faded
snowbird.

MOVING AWAY

I made my way down
to the river
where the poplars
whisper to the water,
and your hand didn't feel
as warm then –
maybe because the water
was moving away.

INSIGHT

Pussywillows rise softly
in coats of fur,
like knives coated with blood.

FOUR

In the morning
where the mist drowns all sight
I see the mist.

Droplets on leaves
cling like a baby's hand
to a finger.

Yellow sunlight
shines in through windows
without clothing.

In the dawn
birds awaken so quickly
insects fear.

AT THE BUSTOP

Sometimes I wonder about you,
and how that China-smooth complexion
manages to last
without cracking or falling apart
until the bustop arrives
in your eyes.

As you gain the stairs
at the usual end of the line,
you always turn back to look,
and your face
is always framed
in the glass and steel
of the folding doors.

Then
I watch as that patulous smile
is snatched from your face
when the bus lurches forward,
leaving me here
to inhale its diesel
and fondle my lunch-bag.

MEADOW LOVE AND MARIANNE

Silently
as time goes,
as the wind throws
itself around us,
cross my lips with yours –

Gently
as the heart goes to sea,
wrap yourself around me,
wear me with pride.

Quietly
as the hurt flees
when we're upon our knees,
love me for long,
love me for strong
in the night that binds us,
in the night that winds us
together.

FOR YOU AND I

For you and I
there are those moments
at the end of day
when the sun
doesn't burn so hard
and the dust is settling
outside.

For you and I
there are thick and thin lines
to bend together.
Nothing can hurt us
or break us in the night-

because
love is the best thing
that we have –

for you and I.

AFTER HOURS

When the sky falls in the evening
and the grass is damp,
it is easier to smell
the lilacs in the backyard
and hear the wind
through the leaves
when the bulldozers are at rest
and the traffic is dying
along the highway.

ABOVE THE ROAD

Sitting here together
in the dusty evening sun
beneath this poplar tree
on the ridge,
I can feel your body,
warm
as your lips on mine,
freeing our love
to the evening settling
along the rutted
and warm dirt road
below.

THOSE CITY FOLK WHO WALK THE MOUNTAIN

I wish to know why it is
that cats can scratch
with greater zeal
while in the dark.

I also wish to know why
you can tear a simple flower
from its roots
without even a little remorse
for the now naked
wound
in the soil.

HOW DO YOU FACE THE STORM

When poplar leaves
turn their silver bottoms
skyward in the wind
just before the rain,
where does your shadow
fall
when you turn your
back,
when you turn it to me.

FIELD

Reel in the miles
of wheatfield,
gold beneath the sun,
and smell the musk
of the black earth
holding it all down
from the sky.

GROWING UP TOO FAST

When children grow up
too fast,
the touch
of too many things
dies,
likewise –
too fast.

Seldom
do they feel the morning
wind
at their skins
when they struggle with traffic
to get to work.

You can seldom sense
the true scents
of their many lovers.

INSPIRED QUICKIE

"I'm tough", said the bully
as he put out the cigarette
with his bare foot,
allowing all his friends to watch.
When he was alone
the next morning
he savored the comfort
of band-aids and salve.

SPREYE

When the dust of day
has settled
and there's no one
in the darkness
to reach out to
beneath a branch-beaten moon,
ride your mare in the mist
and cold spray of breakers
that climb the seawall.

Let the stone train run
its course in front of you
to carry you to the thrust
of the sea.

DRIVEN INTO AUTUMN

When
upon occasion
I miss your eyes
in the October sunlight,
don't worry too long
about the last
moment
we touched.

Your separate dreams
drove me into this
fading condition
of summer ending.

STONE THAT I THROW

When breakers
swell onto the rocks
and soak us
in their agitation,
the stone that I throw
a hundred feet
offshore
sinks
beneath the cast
green
of the flow
of a thousand mountains
distant,
but it does not help keep us dry
against the misconception
of the waves.

CHANGES

A tiny butterfly
bends with his meagre
weight
a stalk of grass,
the very way
that my love for you
has bent
all of the plans
that I cast
for
myself.

MORNING HERO

When left to himself
a hero can become faded
and unnoticed
when he paddles
his canoe
amongst the reeds
in the mist
of an early morning
lake.

TREADING ON DREAMS

I don't like the way
that you bend and break
my grasses
when you walk
through the meadows.

AFTERNOON PRELUDE

When I lay in my rowboat
within the heavy veil
of lake reeds
beneath the hot afternoon
sun
I dream of your wind-shaped
body,
so far away right now.

The taste of the wine
and the water
giggling
against the side
of my boat
brings to me a projection
of the meadow flowers
that I will bring to you
tomorrow,
beneath the same sun.

FINAL STATEMENT

It's taken a long time
for me to learn
that you scoff
at my dreams.

No longer
will I have my wrists
slapped
each time
that I hold a flower.

DOWNSURGE

When the rain falls
it dimples the face
of puddles atop apartment buildings.

It rushes downward
to shatter the tension
by driving everyone
indoors
to leave me alone
with my wine,
with my walking
and rain-soaked face
beneath its umbrella
of fresh tears
and bending leaves.

Swan Lake Junction, British Columbia, 1975

WITHOUT NEIGHBOURS

When all of us sat
huddled
around the campfire
between the rocks
on the lakeshore,
with the wind from the lake
driving the smoke
into our eyes,
there was some kind of rhythm
to the rubbing
and laughter that followed.

Now that we no longer sing
those same old songs
between our spilled beer
and burnt weiners,
and because we have found our own
pathways,
the moon seems heavier
behind each pair
of smoke-stained eyes
because we face the wind
from the lake,
alone,
without those neighbours.

ONE GOOD FIRE

Too many lovers
can leave you as lonely
as mist
in mountain crags.

One good fire
takes away the cold
and stiffness
of many years
of wresting
with such winters.

REACH FOR THE APPLE

When the wind
rolls
the night away
into a hazy, yellow-painted
morning sky,
reach for the apple
by the sleeping butterfly
and dewdrop laden leaf
on the branch.

AFTER THE LONG HAUL

Someone said
that clouds were the nests
that men came home to
after the long haul,
when the wind has broken the ground
into dust
and the sky
pins down the trees
with the airy love
of its expansive chest.

CROSSING

Before you find yourself
beside a stream
saddened
with autumn leaves
give yourself one more
chance
to cross,
barefoot and chilled
to the other side.

BEFORE THE CRISP MORNING

Has your lover
ever taken you
in the darkness
when the roaring mountain
stream
swelled over the rocks
by your campsite,
and the mosquito droned
in anger
around the impenetrable confines
of your tent.

BOND

You've never seen how
an animal and his master
can reach equal terms
until you've seen them both
eating
from the same garbage can.

LOOKING BACK

Were the games
of yesterday
so easy to play,
or were they just moments
purchased
from someone at a price
which was small enough
to let you enjoy
the pride
or the conquest
that rightfully
should never have been yours.

CONTINUITY

The success
of the river
depends
on the mountain's
snow
at its source.

If there was no
winter
there would be but
naked rocks.

DOWNTOWN

I dream of you
often,
perhaps too often.

I wonder if your hand
ever scribbles my name
inadvertently
when you are filling out
your forms
at work.

REMEMBERING ASYA

Meadow grasses
rushed at our legs
as we ran to the bridge
to watch the train
thunder
over the strained timbers
over the creek.

I chased you
and you chased me
in return
until
we finally pulled each other
to each other
in those same grasses
amongst
poplars
when all grew quiet
except for nature's mellow voice.

DEPARTURE

When we met in the subway
where the trains shattered
the air,
you told me
of how you could feel the concrete
shaking
beneath your feet
wherever you walked
so I told you
of the poplars
and wild tiger lilies
in the foothills.

It seems to me
as though your escape
was pre-meditated.

BEYOND THE FENCE

When you climb
a barbed wire fence
and your weight
makes the rusty wire scream
against the nails,
it's nice to alight
in the green barley beyond,
swaying in the wind
where the horizon
is broken
only
by an occasional tree.

LET THERE BE CORRECTION

When the wind roars
through wooded valleys
and pushes waves
over the silk still lake,
I wish it would tear its way
through your hair
and hurl from you
your snotty abuse
and dispassionate laughter.

Burst your way through,
wind.
I say,
let there be a furrow
to channel the storm.

REFER TO MY COLORS

'Treat me well',
said our travelling song,
for more miles
than there are leaves,
but now it is autumn –
everything is on fire
and lovely in the forest,
and that means dying again
for another year.

Press my colors
in your heaviest book,
and when I am green again
in the spring
of next year,
refer to my colors
and treat me well
for autumn comes again,
too soon, into flames.

TIMBER WASTEAGE

When the bit of your axe
bites open the skin
of the tree before you
can you feel sentiment
in some small way
as you watch it bleed,
guilty only
of having brushed the sky
with its branches.

INVESTIGATING A NEW PATH

I thought
that I was doing very well
by placing each foot
in front of the other,
but my feet
were not so accommodating
when I came upon
a large rock.

Was I wise
for stepping around it
or was I lazy
for not jumping over it.

BEHIND

To what voice
do you,
a solemn, better man
plead your case.

There is something here
which does not grow
well –
green, like trees
under the sun,
and I
unlike you
have left it behind
to spawn
with the feathered weeds
under the orange bridge
on Kootenay Lake.

I lost something here
but you are still a hero
and you must sweat
beneath the fact
of having remained
behind
to uphold it.

COMFORT DURING THE STORM

When the storm
bullies the lake
and angers the grass
into ripples
on the hillsides,
come inside by the fire
where fallen pine cones
burn
alongside scavenged wood
thrown up on the beach
by a previous tempest.

SCHOOL 1960

The summer sun
keeps the dust trapped
on the leaves
of wild raspberry bushes
lingering in ditches
and along the fringe of forest.

It's nice to ride the school-bus home
from school
with your friends,
with all of the windows open,
swallowing the dust
from each passing half-ton truck
that rattles by.

WHEN CAROL CAME 'ROUND

When Carol came 'round
she sat herself down
and asked for a smoke.

She had changed,
she had re-arranged herself
into a creature who shone
in a new light
when darkness had prevailed
and drove her into
new terms.

She had left me
to be new
for you,
but you drove her out
as easily as the wind
drives dust
from the easy care
of the earth.

When Carol came 'round
she spoke of you,
of the things that you did
to her
to hide away the wind
from her night.

When Carol came 'round
to cling to our oldness,
she never spoke
of the razor you had used
to shear away
her longing for a simple,
sun-loved, sun-warmed
thing
that she could depend on,
but I felt it.

She cried out in her sleep
at your hatred of the night.
I heard her.

EDITH CAVELL

Evening sun glints
brazenly orange
on the rocky face
of Edith Cavell.

Hereupon
the snows would know
torment
should the spring bloom
early.

TALK

I told Lydia
that we had to talk.

Her reply
was her arms
about my neck.

The roses
have folded for the night
and the moon yearns
for a meadow
from which to speak,
I told her.

Her reply
was the night wind.

PATH

Don't let an angel
of mercy
lure you away
from the peril
of the thorn.

The sleek sword of happiness
is sweetest
when it lies
close
to the heart
and threatens the blood
on its edge.

Between Prince Rupert and Terrace,
British Columbia, 1976

CROSS-TIE WANDERING

The steel of the railway's
twin track
runs a gauntlet of miles
over and through broken stone
and creeping forest.

You and I walked so many
miles
of that trickling steel
stream
with our hands clasped together
that we came to see
those tracks
as our over-seeing father
who bent us together
along the thread of miles
with a wandering sort of
love
that we shared on its many beaches
along its closeness
to the lake.

DAYBREAK

Shadows
are all that remain
of the thick black blanket
of night
that hung over the rocky shoreline
at Ellison Park.

When we loved each other
on those sun-warmed
boulders
the night was with us
softly,
like an enveloping down,
but morning shattered us
with its clean lines
and drove us into the
shadows
between the rocks.

FORMER CHANGE

I don't need a dead leaf
in a stream
to tell me
that autumn has come,
nor do I need
snow
to inform me that
winter
bears down upon yellowing grass.

The sun can shine
as cold in winter
as it can shine warmly
in summer.

THRUST OF YOUR LOVE

When the moon
banishes
its silver
to the wheatfield,
I hope
that,
in some way
it will
thrust
some of your love
to me
where I wait
beneath the stand of poplar
on the rise
near the muskeg.

LEAVING

I can't shut out
tomorrow
when I think about
today.

You thought that you
were being
fair
when you kicked me
but I was the one
who felt the teeth
go.

LOST

Our dictionary
defined you
as a missing autumn
leaf.

I know that you've
flown
because your place on the stem
is vacant
and cold.

THE STREAM BEYOND

This only guitar of mine
is so easy against
the rush and pun
of the water stumbling
over the rock ledge
in the darkness.

I played for you
but met with no
acknowledgement.

If my music does not
rest
in your ear,
let it tumble forth
with the momentary
turbulence
of a stream that is enrapt
in its desperate quest
to escape being smothered
by mountain stone.

SANDSTORM

I heard your heels
click
together
when you danced.

Did you dance for me
or did you merely
appease
the hungry sand
that the winds drive
through the ripening fields
of our plentiful love.

UNITY

Candles
break the night
where we lay
together,
unseparable
beneath these stars.

How is it
that we are so damn
powerful
against the crevass
which has swallowed the others.

NO DENIAL

Paper kites
flirt with the wind
the way
that sunlight wanders in
through my window
to awaken us
with the warmth
of having slept too long.

Imagine us as fabric
which the iron of the sun
bonds
together
where souls aren't denied
their chance.

WITHOUT DEFEAT

When we break down
at last
into old age,
will we still hold the
highway
firmly
in our wandering eyes.

I still want to sleep
in the cold
of the mountains
that scoff
at our temporary
longing
for eternity.

FIRST STORM ON THE LAKE

When the colors
of the lake outside your
cabin
laugh greenly and coldly with
black ice forming,
it is time for the
fire,
of wine and the touch
of the lady who shares
your quilts.

PRESSURE

I was told
that I could choose
between you
and drowning
in the surf.

'How convenient a death
within the tide',
I thought
'How elegant the surf'.

SNOW FALLING

When the lights of the city
are softened
beneath the hazy glow
of snow-bearing clouds
on a winter's night,
streetlights
take on an urgent brightness
beneath the descending blanket
of falling snow.

Many will wake up
in the morning
to a foot of snow
that I watched
fall
silently and unnoticed
for hours before.

THE FINAL YEAR OF BLOOM

You didn't need
your real face
when you were buried
beneath
the spotlight,
but now that everyone
examines you in the same
mirror
you had best buy a new
face
that sports no scar
where the smile
should have been.

RAILWAY HEART

Beating the chaff
from the wheat
was the burden
against starvation
of the farmers
of yesteryear.

How is it
that we find ourselves
beaten now
beneath
this bleaching tyranny
of hidden desires,
concealed from each other
like huge spikes
hidden from every other tie
in the railroad.

PINNACLE

Ever
will our love
brush the sky
when our bodies crush
the grass
beneath its open soul.
Ever will tiny
flowers
blaze against the sun
where our love
meets the gaiety
and clear shine
of the summer sky
above this momental
crag
of our journey
to the highest place
held
within the mountains.

THE FOLD OF THE WIND

When the wind blows
into the midnight windows
as we sit parked
at the head of the
bluff,
the surf below,
I watch your hair wander
breeze-blown
within the vast space
lit
by the moon.
I feel the warmth of your
breath
as a prelude
to the comfort of that blanket
of gentle darkness
that wraps us
together,
for as long as
the touch lingers
within
the fold of the wind.

BETWEEN TIDES

The briny breath
of the sea-swell
bellows in my ears
during the passage
over the boulders.

let us love here
let me take you
before
the next breath
of the intermittent sea
hurls its tidal blanket
upon us,
and buries us
within its memory
of shellfish.

THE SNAKE OF THE WIND

Evening is so smooth,
so candlelight and wine
in this snow-burdened chalet
that the firelight
beckons to the love
within us
beneath its glowing
embers.

When the flames die
and winter winds
snake stealthily
across the roof,
let us be unaware
and closely warm
beneath its frigid breath.

BEACH

The wind cannot see me
when I spread myself thinly
in the darkness.

Shadows
are my only burden
beneath the white-cold
moon
above the beach
where the only drift-wood
bids intrusion.

WHEN WINTER BREAKS BARRIERS

I know
that I must shutter
and brace my windows
against mountain storms
for they would surely
steal
the very fire and spark
from my hearth
should I not enact
my safeguards
against the howling demons
riding the gales.

Let me stay warm
in my clumsiness,
by the fire,
where exploding,
fire-laden logs
dispell the cold
gathered
by the chilling arm
of a relentless wind.

Wells Grey Provincial Park, British Columbia, 1976

WATER-WORN

When the autumn leaf falls
and the swallows abandon
their nests
beneath the old bridge,
I will await you
amongst the water-touched
and polished
boulders
at the shoreline.

Please bring autumn moments
to me
amongst these hard stones
that channel the indifference
of the chaffing currents
of the river.

LAST LIE

Beat the bushes for me
if you will,
but you will only find
that this is the last
time
that I will allow
a lie of yours
to take root
amongst my roses.

RIDGE

Trees
bare of leaf
outline the ridge
like soft strokes
of a charcoal pencil
where we sunk into each other
our love,
and the autumn leaves
now cover
our grassy mattress
for us
until next summer.

TRANSITION INTO MOUNTAIN WINTER

The darkness is cast away
like autumn leaves from a tree
when the alpine night fails
into morning.

Mist settles like a pillow
through the treetops
on the higher slopes
of the mountain
rising above us,
where sometimes
the winds will howl
like starved wolves
on the scent of a lame deer.

STEPPING IN AFTER WORK

Drop by after work
and offer me
your darkness
and stars.

Cool down your anxiety
so that I can taste clearly
the urgency
of the seaweed
in the currents
that swell within
your lips.

PLEADING PRISONER

I have sparks
to hurl against the abuse
of winter
but even the log
has a finite life
against days of bleak
reprisals
of winds
filled with a vengeance.

Hand to me your sword
to cut away
the bindings
of this hateful winter.

BOARDING THE BUS

Each time
that I board the bus
and ask for my transfer,
I know
that that slip of paper
is bringing us closer
to that sought after
touch.

LEAVES

When the trees turn
grey, like wool,
beneath the crowding
winter storm,
the leaves will soon
lay quietly buried
beneath the veil
of coming snow.

KATANA

Choose for me a branch
upon which to escape
the talent
of the clawed beast.

YOUR LIES LIKE LIONS

How may gladiators
have survived the lies
in your bloody arenas.

Are these the lions
that serve you so well
that the spoils dealt to them
become heaped so high
that their feast
continues
on
into every night.

PASSAGE

Touch me where I am
most sensitive.
Touch me where I will respond
to you
the most.

Give me hours
of only your touch.
Let us watch the flames
die away
and go to sleep
slowly.

PROMISES THAT YOU MADE

Where the brook
spills
through your fields,
it leaves behind
bare rocks.

Your streaming forward
to your lofty dreams
has left me to witness
many sun-beached stones.

The grass
has not yet had time
to grow
and to cover
the barren
scars
that you gave so freely.

WHISPER THROUGH

The wind is a variety of
pitches,
of notes and resonances
amongst the naked autumn willows.

Dressed out in our sweaters
in this autumn chill,
the only lingering fingers that run
through your hair
other than those of the sun
are mine.

JENNY

We swam that fifty yards
to the floatation
with its diving board
and lake algae carpet.

There we swam, touched
and made love
under the moon
when everyone else
was snuggly hidden
in their tents in the park.

The water
was icy cold
but our skins burned together
like white coals.

JENNY

You
were the only wind-struck lady
with hazel-yellow,
almost cats' eyes
like mine
that I have ever known.

When we came together
the wind hurried thither,
vent with sparks
about the boulders
of Ellison Park.

We let the wind
douse the flames of our campfire.

From there, our touches
became as dark and mysterious
as the black, lapping waves
which touched near us
beneath an absent moon.

JENNY

You gave love to me
the way that the mountain streams
touch stones, and green grass
flowing within their currents.

Your lips sought mine
as though they were red sparks
against the night.

Your hands sought my love
as though they were vines
about a post.

I sunk my love into you
as though I was the sun
creeping into every crevice,
banishing every shadow,
and you were me
as though you were a meadow
beneath my morning rising.

JENNY

The sough of the wind
through poplar leaves
sounds like the muffled echo
of a raging mountain stream
rushing downhill
in the nearby distance.

At times I believe
that it is you
speaking to me in undertones,
subtle and graceful-
even though you are gone from me
and I am alone with the wind
on this skree
above Bow Lake.

JENNY

Your tongue
was hot and moist against mine
as the sun deserted us
on its day-warmed boulders
and our wind and thick embrace.

The breakers rolled in
to where the shoreline cringed
beneath the late evening,
yet our bodies melted together,
oblivious
to the waves' onslaught
into the heaving sand
and warm evening wind.

MEADOW RUNNER

When my desire
becomes the spirited stallion
between your legs,
recollect the hardness of the leather
reins
which you have drawn
or loosened
to allow me to feed
or to run
amongst the wind-blown
currents
of the wild grasses.

RED

Your kiss
by the trailer
was as sweet
as a brush
of the wind
searching cleverly
through the shocks
of your red hair.

I felt this
within a fleeting moment
and the thought of it
flows over me
as does the cast of a wave
over a pebble.

CHOICE

Had I been offered
the thorn of the rose
and your blossoming heart,
I am not at all sure
that my choice
would come easily.

At present
I prefer the blood-drawing
thorn
to the cut of your
tongue.

ROCKY MOUNTAIN WATERFALL

When the flow
of your icy torrent
rumbles over rocky benches
and disappears
into a filmy
thread
over the final cliff,
it speaks in mist
to the water-cut gorges
meandering away
below.

OUTRIDER

There were dozens watching
when she forced the revs
into the red
and the cliff's edge hurled itself
away
from the screaming motor
and dead foot pedals.

The wind will not hold her
and there will be no more
silence.

SAND RUN

Wrestling with the waves,
with the current and the soft,
giving sand,
you run for my arms
in a fading moonlight
that pursues the black imprints
of your footsteps.

The same, usual
winds
come up salt laden
from the sea
just for the embrace.

ROCKY MOUNTAIN SECRETS

Slim waterfalls
carry down your secrets
from mist-shrouded slopes
to the screes
far below.

They tumble over
and caress the rock
into a pock-marked,
curved smoothness,
until the very tales
or your seasonal wearing
reach and salve my feet
in the rushing exchange
of ice-water
in the pools of your
streams
and torrents.

WILLOW SHORELINE

On that summers's day,
when the sun was hot
on the cool,
willow-sheltered water,
I dreamt of your
arms
about me
in the shadow-ridden
shallows
of the shoreline.

It was not as though
we were making love,
but more of a feeling
of the pulse
of the lake's cast
and ebb.

DEBBIE SIEMENS 1968

When the spring run-off
swelled the creek banks
in Polson Park
we'd run barefoot
through the grass and water
trying to catch frogs.

A half hour later
we were plumbing our brains
for the many solutions
to math class.

I never found many answers.
You never found any clues.

MIDNIGHT STEREO

Stereo lights
beaming across the darkness
of your living-room
are the strongest invitation
to love
upon carelessly strewn pillows
that you will be allowed
by BC Hydro.

INKEEPER

When the warrior
slams down his tankard
upon the oak,
fetch forth the serving
maiden
to quench his thirst
lest he satisfy it
with your blood.

CHRISTIAN

Outside your window
a bird feeds
and sings from your window-box.

Butterflies hover
and deer browse
in the lush greenness of your garden.

The children in your house
cry
and your inner window-sill
bears dead flies as witnesses
to your religion.

CATHOLIC

I brush away the snow
from your window pane
but still
I cannot see inside
to where your love
should be burning.

I am confronted only
with a thin sheet of ice
on the glass
which should boast
the heat of your love.

MEASURES

When you and your lover
sweat together
beneath the moon's caress
and the brush of the wind,
consult my tables
for the weight of your giving,
for your passing into each other.

Measure only the needs
of your hands
upon each other.

RECOGNITION

There is only one sky
to pry into your love.

Share it with the wind
and dust
from where your existence
emerged.

AFTER

When I made love to you
even the waves held their breath
to allow us our peace.

When I look upon you afterward,
the waves
still gather their respect
into total calmness.

WINDS

Tempting were your lips
even when I rushed at them
with my wind.

Tempting still
are your lips
now that the winds are calm.

INNER EXPLOSION

When you arch your back
beneath me,
I think of my cat
who shows her need
to stretch,
having been held too long
within the bond
of sleep
or idleness.

CHEATER

When we exchanged kisses
in the dampness of the swale
in the woodlot,
I compared your lips
to the soft, moist earth,
only to find
that the fungii
had crept into your mouth.

SLIPWIND

Reach out into the shadows
behind you.
Search for the magic
in the dark
where my heart leaps
in respect of fire.

Bare yourself
in the wind of my passing
should the darkness
conceal completely,
my naked desire for you.

OPPRESSOR

You said
that you could tame us,
make us your slaves
beneath your steel.

When the clouds curl up
on the horizon,
I will meet you
with wind;
with my light
I will blind you
from your own blade
and slay you.

ROCKY MOUNTAIN SUMMIT

A broad breath of snow
sweeps
across your rock-strewn face,
like gauze
stuck
to a coarse boulder.

Alpine winds
whip
your exposed skin
as though it was flesh
yielding
beneath the lash.

NIGHT WARRIOR 2

Beneath the moon
the night-warrior scales
the smoothness
of the rock slopes.

The serpent above
awaits
the gleam of the moon
upon the steel
of its foeman
before it considers the strike.

WIND-CLUSTERING

See how my familiar breath
clusters autumn leaves
beneath my passage.

Allow me to stir
your love,
like the leaves,
thickly
into the exposed corners
of my heart.

CONSERVATION

Do not peel back
the bark
from beneath the blossom
for the stem will die.

Leave the bud
to the wind
and the wither of its
sun.

DROUGHT: RELICS IN THE DUNES

Someone spoke to me
damnably of the rain.

There was a time, too,
that I spoke only of sun,
but since then
I have seen many withered
trunks
stretching upward
from the dunes.

OCEAN WAVE

Hold me a little tighter.

Clutch at me
as though you were a wave
washing so very closely
over me.

Move my sandy complexion
in your passing.

Re-arrange me in every way
until we can be patterned
together
in every conceivable meld.

SEA MASTER

You may hail
the slip-sailor
afloat the sea,
but do not expect to hear
a reply
unless the sea should choose
to hurl his prow
toward you
upon its bearing waves.

RUINS

The sunbeam
is a sword of light
that cuts through the dust
suspended in the air
within this cold,
granite tomb.

The energy of serpents
is apparent here
where openings in the stone
glide away
into the cleaner light
of the day above.

VOYAGE

Proudly,
like a gleaming skull,
the ship slips over the waves
toward the furthest edge
of land.

STONE-SLAYER

To discover the secrets
of steel
the warrior must do more
than meditate.

The sun
must warm the metal
wielded by his calloused
dreams.

AID

Help the hand
which is unable to grasp
fully
its sword.

FOUR

Battle lets the swordarm
teach cleavage to flesh
the sun at dusk is crimson-veiled.

In the yellow light of morning
the oceans pick up their pace
pulled by the tide.

Peaches hang heavy on the branch
the pits on the ground attest
to the success of last season.

Mosquitoes sing in chorus
entertaining the wandering beast
whilst chanting for its blood.

ROCKY MOUNTAIN LAKES

Those mountain lakes
which gleam balefully
in this range
are but mere tears
in its stone and ice-pent
history.

GRACE

Grace is not necessarily
the flowing fluidity
of a gentle movement.

It can be the transition
of the fingers
into a squared-off thrust
of a fist.

SUNRISE

Like the jerk of steel
leaping toward the throat
of its foeman,
the sun arcs its slash
of whiteness
across the morning horizon.

BEFORE YESTERDAY

When you look upon your mirror
and read the careful lines
of your face,
can you still deny the fact
that your ancestors
may have held bloody hearts
freshly cloven and stolen
from the heaving chests
of relatives.

YOUR BEST ATTITUDE

Is it true to say
that the weather here
is your only voice.

Are you thus,
always this cold
and forever ice-laden.

CHURCH-GOER

The organ wails
within the hollow stone walls
of your cathedral.

You can no longer taste
the resplendent, swivering
beauty
of the butterfly,
perched on the gentle sway
of wind-woven grasses.

Has your religion
locked you so completely away
for so damn long.

GLADIATOR

The hollow of your mind
is merely an echo
of the arenas
of yesterday.

Somewhere
within that space of time
your hands drew the blood
of those who were too thick-headed
to rationalize swiftly.

FIVE

Roots creep outward
freed from the musty soil
the sun's heat burns.

Leaves spin from autumn branches
and land on cool swirling water
rushing away downhill.

Sun bakes raw clay into stone
the potter fashions the mud
and returns it to the sun.

Snow melts slowly
the sun takes its time
in freeing the ground.

Purity exists
before rainwater mixes
with dust.

IN PRAISE OF DRAFT HORSES

Measured and heavy
are the footfalls of the heavy horse
who pulls the stoneboat
laden with rock
from his master's fields.

Praise the work horse
for his part
in allowing us to plant our seed
in the soil,
broken and cleared by his sweat,
that we will use forever
after he is spent and gone.

O'Keefe Ranch, British Columbia, 1976

CLIMBER

When the moon
laughs
down at the black,
Rocky Mountain monoliths
hulking beneath
its steely gleam,
I, too,
laughed.

When I urged my aching body
over cleft after vertical cleft,
I quickly lost my mockery
after gazing
into ever-deepening
rock-crowded abysses
below me.

FACE VALUE

Don't be flattered
when the moon is appropriate
for us.

It may be gleaming
for some other couple
locked
in the throes of love
in some field
where their thoughts
and breaths
are solely for each other.

HANDS UPON YOU

Could armor be justice
or compromise
to the arrow.

Could my hands upon you
be some form of need
or could it merely be
the force of many winds
thrusting against my elbow.

CLIFF

A thin bed of pine-needles
graces the cliffside clefts
beneath the occasional pines
which lean out
foolishly
over a thousand-foot
precipice.

TIME, LIKE LOON-SONG

When a new wind
ruffled the grasses
on our sun-burned slopes
and the spray of the waves
left us still hot
beneath the moon,
a new day was always there
to spread away our energy.

Now that the loon sings
within the mist of morning,
the sun no longer needs
its usual hurried chance
in order to rule.

BRAND

When you shield the light
to get undressed
and the night begins
with a moan,
I hope for you
to complete your chrysalid
transformation
within my arms.

When your gentle
cries
succeed the winds' soughing,
you will have become
the night brand
which I have sought
for my own skin.

HORSEMAN

Do not corner my needs
behind your wagon.

When your horses
surge foreward
against the frail green
of the hills,
leave not behind
my desire
to be your horseman.

WHILST BOUND

How often does frost
come
to the rose
in summer.
How often
does my touch
stray
from your breasts
whilst my thoughts
are bound
securely
by the warm sand.

BETWEEN PROOFS

When my pages
are fully bent
and my company seems to hide away
my lonliness,
don't ask for an answer
in my black clouds.

Let me touch my lips
to yours
that I may fool
the brewing storm.

BENEATH THE CRUST

The Pika
cowers
beneath heavy boulders
split asunder
by the icy caress
of mountain winters.

Somewhere
below the rock
lies a dry, grass nest,
still warm
against the fury
of the changing wind.

CROSS-ROCK JOURNEY

The mountain sheep
runs at ease
where my eyes
cringe
amongst the rocky
cliffs.

Even the simple
lichen
would fare better than I
in a tumble
down this talus ladder.

WITH THANKS

I am he
who bears his sword for you
against the fear
that echoes
in your dream-torn night.

I smote each dragon
whose evil smile
burned away your best days,
yet you repay me
with an ashtray
full
of spent cigarettes.

SURGE 2

When your harness
snaps beneath the burden
and you surge free,

find my channel
and surge toward me.

SURGE 3

Give to me that moon
so brazen upon your shoulders.

Give to me that wine
so bold upon your lips.

Neither one of us are kittens
interested only
in soft-woollen playthings.

SEARCHING

Something you said
led me to a fountain
which sprayed forth
only lilies.

When I searched
the blackened water
for a clue
you gave me but petals.

I strain against my oars
for the scent
of even the water.

PRELUDE

When your branches
wear the wind
from a midnight lake evening,
send the softened
swell
of a wind-driven wave
to round and shape
my lips
to your breast.

MOUNTAIN FOREST

Broad mushrooms
fan outward
from amongst rotten
logs
and green horsetail.

The spent leaves
of yesteryear
still linger
in the cool moistness
of the forest floor.

LOVE SONG

When the minstrel wears
the wind
that seeks our hair,
I'll play for you
my love song
that it be compared to fair
flowers.

LOVE WARRIOR

Send forth your drummer
to play his wistful tune.
Send to me your wind-scattered
leaves
to mask away the moon.

Bring to me a sun
that will burn away the
mist;
bring down the silky veil
of rain that hid away
each time that we kissed.

Bend toward me
your many foeman
that sweep away the moment
and I will slay them
with my blade.

ISABELLE

A poem
is what I wished
to spell for you
but the weight
of my hand
can come closer
to your heart.

SUSAN CLAY (VERSE 1)

How roughly
or how deeply
must my fingers cleave you
to solicit a response.

SUSAN CLAY (VERSE 2)

Yestertime
you were
such a damn fine lady.

Such roses fade
you've shown me.

Oh where did my stream touch
such distant and colder stones
that you would refuse
the very grass and mud
from my summer banks.

SUSAN CLAY (VERSE 3)

The -57° Fahrenheit
winter night's journey
to the outhouse
where huge ice crystals
lurked upon the seat
awaiting my bare skin
was not so difficult
as trying to figure out
why you turned out
the way
that you did.

SUSAN CLAY (VERSE 4)

Reach into this void
that you call a relationship
and show to me
that which your hand has grasped.

SUSAN CLAY (VERSE 5)

Shannon had the music,
Amber held my rose.
Robin could reach me
in any state
but you had your whole hand
in your nose.

SUSAN CLAY (VERSE 6)

How far into this earth
does the sun thrust its warmth

I measured you
and found you to be colder
than the ore
in the minds of most miners.

SUSAN CLAY
I WON'T BE THERE
(VERSE 7)

I won't be there
when your sun splashes
into the sea.

I won't be there
when your new love fails
to thrust the wind
into your bedroom window.

I won't be there
to hold you
when you are defeated
by trivia.

I won't be there with my love
or the dreams that I had
for the two of us.

I won't be there.

SUSAN CLAY (VERSE 8)

I've found a new life-
one which touches you
only slightly.

I have my confidence.
I have my wind.
I have my mountain flowers,
which strain toward me
when I pass by.

RAINSTORM

Spirit away the dust
with your heavy tears.

Allow once again
the dusty leaf to breathe
beneath the windy cleansing
of your fury
whence beneath which
the dust of yesterday's wind
has been slain.

SNOWSHOE

This shining lake
becomes a snow-laden mirror
in winter.

Here,
the imprints of snowshoes
may reveal any pathway
chosen
by those who finance
their journeys
with snow.

SLIPSTREAM VOICE

Upon the leaf
a dewdrop shines
almost as gleamingly
as your eyes.

Below the bridge
tumbles
rock-harried
water,
murmuring
as does your voice.

Jets roar overhead.

MARSH-LAKE MORNING

When the morning sun
burns away the mist
and peers onto our tent
pitched on a headland
crest,
don't roll over
before kissing me the way
that the night
wrapped
our canvas.

WIND ROAMING UPON SAND

When we roam the beaches
within the wind,
beneath the soft
blanket
of night,
stars burn white
as though
reflecting
the occasional words
we utter.

OVERWIND CRESTING

When your hands
grasp me
and caress me
my fires swell to the edge
of my breath,
waiting to lay you
barren
within your weeping
joy
beneath the powerful sweep
of the coming wind.

BUBBLES

Have you ever seen
bubbles rise,
drifting up in a close column
from an unknown source
at the bottom
of a pond.

Would you ever
permit
my hands
to arise within you
the frothy, white
bubbles
of seeping love
as they wander over your body
where
it is warmest.

DISCARDS

When I count
the beer cans,
the cigarette packages
and refuse
from the polaroid cameras,
I wonder
how long it will take
to love these
damn fine mountains
to death.

NUNNATOK (B.C.)

This hulking black
fist
defies
even simple grass
and the old glaciers
which nudge at it
from two sides.

It peers down
on simple pines
and worn old rock
partially hidden,
thither and you
amongst lingering spring snows.

WATCH WITH ME THE CATTAILS

Watch with me
as the cattails sway
in the wind.

Watch with me
the way their feather light
seeds
waft away
after they burst free
of their velvet cloak.

Watch with me
the pride of their barren
stems
as they stand,
spent,
until the winter's frost
bends and snaps
the dried, rigid sternness
of their spines.

SUNSOARING

The daylight beyond the night
beckons to us
to unfold our wings and soar
sunward
from our perches
on this decaying city's plateau.

FORTUNES

When you slap your wallet
to verify your coins,
don't count on me
because I will be counting
the crests of waves
from the hillock.

SLUMBER-MELT

Pussy-willows
are the harbingers
of spring,
until then the snow
enjoyed
its many months slumber
amidst stones,
upon grass and leaves.

WOOD-VIOLETS

Within the moistness
of the woods
in mid-June,
the wood-violet raises its
dampened face.

It speaks forth
from broad leaves
where rotting trees
stretch away into
moss
and lichens.

LINE BETWEEN CHOICES

The grass
is more supple
nearer to the shade,
but here
where my soul thrives best,
the winds howl longer
and colder
in winter.

ON TRAPPING

If you were to feel
the steely vise-grip
of your traps,
upon your wrist,
you would destroy your traps
and befriend my hatred
of traplines
to benefit your love
and respect of the animal
whose dead and frozen eyes
are wiser in too many ways
than yours.

PROTECTION

Where the sword flows
airborne,
so does blood and bone.

Mine edge
is of the keenest steel,
and darkness
will stray and waste thither
for me
after my curving arcs.

FAMILY

Where hands grasp
in embrace
there must be
the close caress of the wind.

Where hearts coincide
there must be
the desire
to show love.

When it comes to family
all things must be
held
within
such a wind's tossing
of bluff grasses.

JOURNEY

Little
can deceive me
from this pathway
of destiny
save for a twisting cobble
that lends to mist
which obscures one's sight
of ruffians
and cut-throats
in worn alley-ways.

DUSTY OLD MEN
SHOULD MAKE NO RULES

Can I crush you
closely
to me
because you are family,
or should I worry
about friends,
or the laws
which govern us
that love-making must not
be
for you and me
because we share common blood.

COMING THROUGH SLOWLY

This town doesn't look so well
in snow
because you have not
as yet
consented
to melt my needs
into moistened spring.

ROCKY MOUNTAIN PAUSE

Centuries
of building scree
spreads out
like a wide fan
upon this slope
whereupon
we've paused
to embrace and touch,
and stare at the sweep
of the valley
below.

HARVEST

Heavy
blow the winds in September.

Fields glint
golden
beneath Alberta sunsets.

Derelict farmhouses
stand like ageless stone
amidst swaying fields
of wind-driven oats.

The sundown submits
to the grain-field
like a horizon smitten
by a fiery red sword
which slashes back
the horizontal color
with the varying degrees
of sun-proven blood,
bled from the harvest of the land.

Otter Lake Road, British Columbia, 1976

JASPER VALLEY STREAM

In this high
valley
the stream takes its time
whilst writhing
amongst
yellow wild-flowers.

These alplands
cry and suffer
little
from the rusting
hulks
of battered automobiles.

BLACK GROW THE SKIES

Through my window
I watch the prairie sky
blacken
into crushing storm.

I feel the sweep
of moisture-laden wind
rush through my screen-door.

At last
I see the lightning
sear the sky
from horizon to horizon
as the downpour begins
its angry passage to the soil
of the fields
around this farmhouse.

Marlene Clay

BEYOND MOSS

You showed up
to visit me
after a trying day,
and coming together
eased away the hardness.

My only fear
is that you will forget
me
after tomorrow is spent.

MOUNTAIN LAKE AUTUMN

When the sunset
burns orange
above the tree-line,
our rowboat
shielded amongst reeds
is our haven.

Here, the bottle of wine
and our loving
flow freely
beneath the autumn chill
and the fleeing arrow
of Canada Geese
overhead.

NIGHT WIND'S PASSING

When you made
love
to me
I burned colored candles
into the wind
which set to moving
the curtains to the night.

When you shuddered
beneath me,
the curtains billowed
and the wind roared
in the darkness.

AS DOES THE TIGER

A kitten
stretches
and flexes
her claws
as does the tiger.

The subtle difference
is that the kitten
knows not yet
of the blood taste
of the mouse
as does the tiger.

TOWARD SPRING

Snow,
freshly fallen,
caps
the stones of the stream
and the stumps
of the winter woodlands.

Only mist
will serve to break
the dull coldness
of a muchly warmed
winter's day
approaching Spring.

THIS PINNACLE

Akin to sun-warmed
boulders,
your breasts are full
and heated to my
touch.

When I sink
into you
and your warmth
clutches at me
in return,
let there be an
understanding
between our flesh
that flourishes
on these wave-swept
touchings.

THREE

A blazing fire
heats the black air
that has grown from shadows.

Let the embrace
become one common groan
between us.

Save my leaf –
press it between the pages
of your heart.

BEACH FIRE

When the fire burns
and the lakeswell churns
beneath the wind,
may we e're relive
this firelight and wave.

GIVEN

I've given you roses
when the wind was heavy
on a grey day.

I've given you my love
when the river fled past
in a washing way.

ONE

Daylight fades
like the yellowing
of paper.

SPRING AWAKENING

Snow en-crusted boughs
drape, wind-ravaged,
over the sleeping badger below.

When the buds swell
along the river banks,
the creatures which have lain
silent
all winter
will be aprowl in the water-beds
before the wind soughs warmly
through the later-blooming reeds
and grass.

COULD YOU KEEP ME
TO SOFTERSTONE

Every night
that you find me
windswept
you will find me
nestled
between cloud and stream.

If you could see
how I feel,
you'd know how I
deal
with stone.

COUGAR

The reach
of the cougar
does not rest behind the
veil
of winter's cloak.

Beware
the thick branches
of the pine
and of the rock
outcroppings
which may house
the future forms
of his stealth.

ANGIE

You are so graceful,
so supple;
you touch me like a breeze.

We met only weeks ago
and the interim
has been fire.

TRANSITION

Don't tell me
of how the stream stones
hurry downhill
behind the onslaught
of the current.

Rather,
tell me of how
the autumn leaves
sail the water's surface
to a point
where the stream
blends
into river.

FORMER LESSONS

I lent my hand,
outstretched,
to a deer
in a grove
of poplar saplings
and it fled
into the brush.

I do not feel hurt
because it bethought itself
of the snarl or the raking claw
of a previous predator.

SEARCH

When the earth opens up
to swallow known stones,
can you blame my love –
like an earthquake –
for probing
into your very heart
for consideration.

SEARCH 2

Seek me
where the eddy curls downward
'neath
the bridge.

Seek me
amongst
brightly colored stones
polished by mud.

WITHIN THE PRAIRIE STORM

Oft
have you been
within
the storm.

Have you understood
its wind
and its need
to stretch
away
o'er prairie grain
where yellow crops
touch
such a black
sky.

TWO

Leaves fall in blankets
where summer lovers brushed
against the stream's stones.

Put away your book,
put away your pen and
release our pages from light.

CLOSING TOGETHER

My eyes are wide
when you come nigh.
My heart is a sea-swell rhythm
when I hear you sigh.

OBSERVATION 2

There are those
I suppose,
who never do
have a clue.

OBSERVATION 3

Cars
parked in winter rows
in immense parking lots
resemble a wheat-sheaf
line
of dominos
coated with snow.

OBSERVATION 4

A dead yellow leaf
crushed and trapped
beneath a thick layer
of transparent ice
is like a sheet
of newspaper
which has been trod upon
tenfold,
and left to the trappings
of the wind.

OBSERVATION 5

Ice
clings to the hydro wires
like a dozen jetstreams
in the cold, blue sky
above.

OBSERVATION 6

Stars wink in the night sky
like eyes blinking
at some bright light
thrust into its black face.

CONTRACT

I am sure
that the torrent
has an agreement
with the stones
beneath its passage,
just as the meadow-grass
knows of the inevitability
of frost
upon its yellowing blades.

THIS SWALE IS OUR KEEP

Every night we spend
beneath these unknown poplars
lends to some sunlit hint,
some message or prelude
to a warmer tomorrow.

The creek nearby
has always been -
so has winter's
barren rage
but this fire,
like eternity,
will burn
within this circle of stones
laid by our hands.

UNABLE TO SEE YOU

Some have said
that my heart holds
an illusion
of love
when I hold
you.

Some who have known you
have said that you
put out
fire
with misty breath,
and that concealed hate
for love
is some raw
and untouchable anger
within you.

LAYKE SPREYE

I jerkt the
tiller
and the wynd
slapt our sayls
taut.

Hykt out
o'er the gunnale
we felte the
spreye
from the bowe
as we rayct
headlong intewe
our loving
wynd cresting
and wyte wayves.

WAVERIDERS

'Let go
the tiller',
she cried.

Her feet slipped
from the toe-strap
and she crushed my
lips
with a kiss
as the sailboat
fed into the wind
and stopped still,
the sails slack
and wind-ruffled.

FROST AND US

Leaves
sketch diagrams
by falling in autumn.

The colorings and shapes
are barely symmetrical.

You've never let me down
when the same autumn leaves
have cringed,
uncovered
beneath the near winter
autumn night's frosting.

BOB

When you fought
with your lover
in my truck
while I was driving you
home,
and punched me in the face
when I protested,
I felt good
somehow
by dragging you
from the cab
and reddening the ground
outside
with your blood.
My friendship
also knows limits.

Marlene Clay

SPENDING TIME TO SAND

I'll come running
if you need to love me.
I'll gather the wind
about us.

Grasses
will be glad
to bend beneath us.

Stay with me
until the fire
burns to ash.
Keep with me
until mountains
crumble.

MORNING

It's hard to leave you
in the morning
to go to work.

It's hard to leave you
laying there abed,
yearning for more
waves.

MORE OFTEN

The closeness between us
is getting
closer.

Our fingers clutch
more tightly
and our chests
touch
more often.

We anticipate
these meetings
more often
and the heat from
coming together
like this
will melt into one
shudder,
also, more often.

NIGHT EBBING

Indentation near wet sand rim;
footsteps follow
in the strand,
still safe from
curling waves.

Strike down the
moon
in preparation
for another
morning.

FIREBRINGER

'Years are wafting away
like windborne smoke',
said Sarah.

She drew aside the curtains
and stared,
candlelit
into the shiny street
below,
made silver-white by rain.

Her hair moved
faintly
in the breeze.

Then
she turned,
set down her glass
and brought
fire
to me.

DEWMORN

Dewmorn
is thick in this glade
from whence night is preparing
to flee.

Everywhere are signs of deer,
of coyotes and quail
in the mud.
Water drips as quicksilver
from ferns and broad bush.

Night
is gathering its greying rags –
fading into the distance
whilst I stand shivering
in its wake.

FADING

The sidewalk wears you
somehow,
with a pride not found
in rain-pools.

Reflections
of such a yesterday
remain in yellowed photographs
stuck with pins
to the wooden trim
of your bureau-glass.

Can you still find
aught else amongst roses
than their thorny greetings.

FOOTHILLS STORM

The sky
was blue-black
when I tossed aside
my half of the quilt
this morning.

The fire
soon roared
hearth-pent
while the storm
outside
raged
and set this old
cabin
to shudder.

I'm glad that you were here
to share
these storm-loosened leaves.

WINTER'S EVENINGS

I spent hours most every night
at my typewriter
punching away at the book
that might have made us famous,
and you sat there with me
rubbing my shoulders
just to be close.

The book lost itself to crumpled paper
but your hands were still there
touching me.

ACKNOWLEDGEMENT

When we are lying
in each others' arms
and our guns go off together,
we should somehow
acknowledge
our bodies
for their arrangement
of curves,
and the skin that heats us.

BIG CITY

Wondering
at what magic I see
in this city
where the air on the horizon
is yellow-brown
and filthy,
is like asking why
pigs
lay down in shit.

KAREN HORNBY
NELSON, BC

When
after skating
I walked you home
and you kissed me
for my efforts,
I still hear the
snow
crunch
beneath my boots
as I in turn
walk home.

It seems as though
I am still walking
home
though
it's years later and we've lost touch.

NIGHT RAIN
NELSON, BC

When the rain slick
on Baker Street
reflects
the colored glare
of the shoplights and streetlamps
at night,
my journey to the Queen's Hotel
will hold more than the taste
of a beer
with friends.

KOKANEE SPAWNING
NELSON, BC

We watched the Kokanee
spawn
in the dark,
almost black
shallow pools
of a near dead stream
in the provincial park.

Near-autumn grasses
blanketed the banks
whereupon rested
the bloated remains
of proud fighting fish
left to doom by a mother
who was busy weaving summer
into autumn.

BAD AUTUMN DAY

Coarse yellow grass
rises
like stiff hair
from the scalp
of the meadow.

Autumn
and its chill
sure can fuck up
meadow-grass
dreams
near winter.

SUN JOURNEY

In the ponds below this tree
the sun has cloven
its westward way
with wide swashes
of steel
upon the water.

DUST DROWNING

When the sky
shudders
within its color
and the rain bursts
through cloud-slits,
compare the drowning
dust
to the frenzy
of angry serpents
roiling in the thick, dirty
grass
at the roadside.

COMING

Bring to me
your nakedness
as though
it were the scent
of coming snow
on the wind.

Vernon, British Columbia, 1977

EVENING JOURNEYS

The shocks
of your blond hair
spill down against my face.

Walking to your
grandfather's old house
in the freezing mirth
of winter
led me up steep streets
of shining ice
and lawns boasting
of freshly fallen snow.

I think
perhaps,
that I did not come
often enough.

MOUNTAIN

Snow,
like dust,
chokes the gaping
wounds
between boulders
upon the scree.

Send forth more rubble
for me to scramble.

MOUNTAIN 2

Snow
coats your skin
like a watercolor
wash
on museum rag.

THE ICE CAVES

The day was of ice crystals,
of laughing,
of long branch shadows
and crushed snow.

Our trail followed
the dried, buried vein
of the creek,
and the crackle of the fire
in the cave mouth
was like the wind
vanishing
across rooftops.

THE ICE CAVES 2

Hide away the tears
that you bleed
for the stream.

When your feet
plunge through the snow's crust,
leave a footprint
which is shallow enough
to fool the spring melt.

LEND ME YOUR HEART

Weave for me
the strongest web
of your love.

Seize me thoroughly
as though I was a stem
within a breeze.

Ever renew
my soul's taste
for such a gift.

VALENTINE 1980

If only I knew
the way to touch you
as fragrantly
as flowers bloom.

STONEHENGE

When the lightning
seared the black air
around the megaliths
of Stonehenge,
did the blood curdle
upon the altar.

Was the knife arrested,
poised.

Did the women shriek
and the warriors run
when the wind
roared
through the circle,
casting angry firebrands
and rain-pelt
under a black sheet
of cloud.

WIND ON THE CLIFFS

Don't break down for me.
Just give me your flow.
Hold me as close as waves
hold sand.

TOMORROW'S ROSE

Raise again my goblet
to your lips.

Drink
of my white love.

In a year
you will know me
mayhaps
the way the rose
craves
rainfall.

UNTITLED

I didn't see you
for a whole weekend.

I felt like a single petal
on a bloomed-out flower.

I felt like a wind
which had no shoreline
upon which
I could thrust waves.

AT THE MOMENT OF SUNSET

When the sun
burns redly
as though it was a skull
sinking
for the last time
into the sea,
melt upon me
as though I was all
that was left
of anything
before the final moment
struck.

AFTER THE LIGHTS

When your wetness
soaks me in anticipation
of my blooming,
I will wear you
as fully
as my petals
wear
the sun's hotness.

HAY-SWEET

When,
with rage,
the wind shakes the leaves
of the poplars
rush to the lee of the haystack
where my opposing love
will lay you gently bare
of driven rain
and coldness.

HEARTS

Hearts
are like leaky buckets
which can hold only
part
of the river's flow
of wisdom.

PRESERVATION

The dance
of the flickering candle
is as finite as petals.

This mountain torrent
will last for as long
as we leave it alone
to caress its pebbles.

THE CITY GROWS UP

Through my window
I watch the city grow up.

I see the cranes
reefing on buckets of concrete
as the shells of towers
slowly take form.

In their shadows
I see the sun banished from gardens
and the wind channelled
through solemn avenues.

Soon the grass will be gone,
replaced by paper bags and boxes
being blown along the pave.

MEADOW

Cars stream along these streets
as do currents in the river.

Somewhere,
in some field are horses
which do not know
the whine of a motor
nor the grey pave that rings
to the fall of their shoes.

SUSAN CLAY

There's something about the
storm
that I have never
liked.

Perhaps
it may be you.
I detest the way that you
cringe
before its cleansing.

SEPARATING, 1979

How can these days
pass
without some form
of love-bond.

How dare we awaken
after all this time
to cool breeze
and yellow sun
without at least
a kiss.

END OF MARRIAGE

Silence and empty time,
like waves
caresses the boulders
where once our love
flowed,
seeping into every crack–
brushing each tiny stone
and grain of sand aside
with its froth.

HOW YOU DREW ME IN

Your love drew me to the sea
where mist,
like a poem
took me in
and gave me to you
in such a madness
that we became sea-froth and sand
together.

DIRT ROAD IN SPRING

When the road
trails away into ruts
through the trees,
thank the sun
that it didn't melt you
instead of the early spring snow.

Thank the thaw
that your heart is not leaving
like the frost
now shedding the soil
that harbored it.

ASCENT TO THE ICE CAVES

My boots
caress the slant
of your storm-peeled rock.

Give me purchase
for my feet and my hands
in my design
to reach the pleasant curve
of your mouth.

When within your grasp,
give me the valley-view
that I seek.
Give my pounding heart
and coursing blood a chance
to blend
with your cold splendor.

ACCIDENT

Throngs gather, curious
about the creased body
bleeding on the ground.

The bumper
wears a tremendous dent.

Sirens wail in the distance
as someone yells out,
"Fuck off,
this ain't no social gathering".

The crowd moves back
and the lifeless body
feels again
the breeze coursing over it
as its child weeps
in another's arms.

AUTUMN BOOK

I've moved my way
through most of the old book.

It said nothing
of raging mountain water.

It spoke only of dead lovers
and grass
beneath wide trees.

It did not give me peace.

It did not give me flowers
to garnish my valleys.

The only thing I remember
is a dead leaf
in the brook.

This is not a plot
but there certainly is
a motive.

FLAMES BY THE BOATS

Take me home lovely lady
to the flames by the boats.

LIST OF PERSONAL DEMANDS

Whisk me away on your wind
to where the poplars burn
as yellow flame
in autumn.

Give me back my chilly autumn
farm mornings,
that I might raise clouds of mist
with my breathing.

Return to me the arrows
of Canada Geese
that cut the sky in their urgency
to be gone.

Give me back my long grass freedoms.
Give me back my wood smoke
and rustling leaves
which I share with the sky.

HOMEWARD

Ware ye, stranger
for I'm bound to a road
paved with nothing more than dirt.

It leads through poplars
into more poplars,
through damp swale
and ribbon of creek
to a meadow of tall grass.

Ware ye, stranger
for should you blink your eyes
and take them from me,
I will disappear forever from you
into that poplar fence
and curtain of leaf
for only I know what lies thither
and t'is where I'm bound.

SILENCE HERE
WILL NE'ER SOUND
THE SAME

These lovely poplar,
heavy yellow and mottled
in autumn
are doomed in the winter
when they will fall to the
axemen.

Take
your fucking lumbar company
out of my woods.

SARAH

When our bellies touched
and our warmth
melded into ripples
beneath the moon's sweep
on the bluffs of Ellison Park,
we had the play of the lake waves
for music.

Oft came we here
and our final parting
wore no stones.

Some part of us will cling thickly
to that stone depression
in the cliff,
hidden from all else
beneath those many summer moons.

CATHY POEGMOELLER

I saw Cathy's grave
today.

They finally put
a headstone on it.

Though no one hears her,
she is still yelling at the game
when the puck slams
into the boards,
and the check
is followed by blood from punches
and the ice is littered
by gold gloves and sticks.

VERGE OF MORNING

At times
the night can be
too goddamn short.

How can I show you
any expression of love
when the sun
thrusts itself
into the tent
and rips my eyes
away from the lovely blackness
of yours.

STORMS

Like smoke,
clouds crowd the summit
of Mt. Robson.

If the furies of these storms
were as swords
mountains would be as dunes.

AUTUMN TO WINTER

Blanket me
with a soft kiss
of yellow leaf.

Cover my stream
with a quilt of ice.

WINTER FARMYARD

The yardlight
gleams coldly
in the still
snowflaked air
of the winter's night.

The woodpile
cowers beneath snow.

TO ROCKY MOUNTAIN HOUSE

The old red Chev pickup
always made the trip
to Rocky.

I can almost see
the wind
flowing over the curved hood
while granny swept
the sleep from my eyes
with spit
on her handkerchief.

AUTUMN COVER

A leaf
turns,
colored
within its downward
autumn
journey.

It does not condemn
the breeze
that lowers it
to the ground
which will soon wax more coldly
beneath winter's haste.

STORM NEARING

I look to the way
the storm
swallows the distance
inside
of its blue-black belly.
I crave the way
that the crops gleam and ripple
in variant green tones
beneath the mounting wind
and sunstrike.

Barkerville, British Columbia, 1976

DISCARDED TRACTORS

The sun weaves a yellow swath
beyond the outhouse
where the barley ripens
into gold
and old tractors
rust,
towed to a corner of the field
and forgotten
to snow and the ravage
of dust-wind,
of bird's-nests
and the seasons' caresses.

SOUS LE PONT

Meet me 'neath
the bridge
where
slats of light
shimmer dust-ridden
about us.

Kiss me here
where this bare soil bank
counts its days
just feet away
from rushing water
and huge stones.

HUNGERING

Is it wiser to hunger
for love
and a gentle touch
or to hunger
for bread and wine.

CRAVING

Wolves thirst after the blood
of deer
as does the sea
thirst
after stones.

BLESSINGS

Count your blessings
for you will not know how many
you have
until you run
hopelessly short
of fingers.

Marlene Clay

JANICE

Outside,
snow
continues to swirl
wind-harried.

Pretend no longer
that we do not share
the same taste
that driven snow
has
for porous, cracked stone.

WINTER WATERFALL

Ice clings
like fur
to the rocks and trees
surrounding
the winter waterfall.

Water becomes mist
and freezes upon itself
to form a bearded
white statement
upon the whisperings
and murmurs
of the creek,
whilst the pebbles
shiver
below.

OIL

Derricks
crouch
on Alberta's fertile skin,
probing deeply,
hungrily,
for its black blood.

SHIPS ON THE NOD

When your ships
are on the windsweep of the lake waves,
surge their prows
toward me
that I might watch
their timbers gleam past me
beneath the sunstrike.

COURSING

The sough of the wind
through the reed beds
is somehow remissful,
though the wind
cares little for the bending
of others.

Sometimes
the wind is merely gentler
than stones.

ARRIVING AT KINNEY LAKE

At the end of the trek
I was held solidly
by the azure-blue
glacial melt-water
that wound its way 'neath
the peeled log bridge
and on to rock-harrying
and foam.

OUT ON THE EVENING

When the streets
are aswirl with leaves and dust,
walk with me here
in the evening
when it is warm
and the sun renders the horizon
as a red breath
fading to yellow.
My hand on your shoulder
and yours about my waist
are the kinds of touches
that the air has for leaves.

RIVER RUNNING

My heart is as close
to you
as is the moon
that spills down
into the river
that runs as gleaming
oil
through the night.

STONEBOAT RIDER

A powerful, black
Percheron
pulls stoneboat and farmer
burden
past a hay raker
choked by drifting snow.

Great clouds of
vapor
from hard worked
nostrils
explode in the air
and disappear
within
the prairie wind.

WHILE THE SKY THUNDERS

These blankets of cloud
roil
and turn in upon each other
like sheets about lovers,
while the sand
and valleys far below
rest
beneath the lack of detail
which has been snatched away
by the darkness.

OUT FROM UNDER THE WING

Those pebbles
ground beneath the raging
of the water,
fast and free and wide,
are being given their only
chance
to journey into sand.

A stone
cannot rest for long
'neath the wing of the mountain.

ON THE CURRENT

Children
dragging their paper boats
along the gutter
fall down and skin their knees.

There are no tears
for the boats are yet afloat.

SHUSWAP MORNING
UPRIVER FROM MARA LAKE

When the tree-trunks
are sodden black with moisture
and morning mist swirls steamily
only inches
above the river,
the cry of the Great Blue Heron
pierces the damp stillness
to herald morning.

It is time to progress further
upriver
where the osprey clings
to its stick nest atop a dead tree
until the sun burns a blue swatch
in the sky.

WEAR ME (AUTUMN)

Autumn dons its fiery costume
of heavy, burning colors,
much the same as my skin
dons yours,
in the mottled tone
of melding together.

Wear me
as the autumn ground
wears its cover of flames.

Search me out
whenever the wind rustles
your leaves.

Blanket me thickly.

SEA

Should that light
go out in your heart,
I guess that it would be
sorry and heavy waves
for me.
Do not let me be washed away
from you
as seaweed and empty shells
in the swell and ebb.

Give my sands
purchase
to your shores.

TEACHER

You should not have been
a teacher.
You knew too little of waves
and spitballs.

You knew nothing
of the changes of the seasons
as I know them.

The fear of ice
gives you to cringing
before any burning fires.

You have no meadow
to fly to.

GROWING OLD
(A POEM OF LOVE AND THANKS)

There is no fantasy
involved
with going grey and growing old.

I've tried
but I cannot break free.

I'll grow older
and love you more
for other reasons
once the grace of your body
is gone
and your hair is grey-granite stone.

I'll always love you
because you gave mountains
to me
when we had youth
and autumn leaves and wind.

EDITH CAVELL

The north slope
of Edith Cavell
wears Angel Glacier like a necklace.

For how long
can the stone rise up to meet
the caress of the ice.

FREE THE STONES TO SAND

Free the stones
imprisoned in the mud.

Let them roll and pitch
freely
within the rage of the stream.

Give to them
the width and the course
of the river-bed
to become the sand at the sea
in which you and I
make love.

CASTLE MOUNTAIN

You thrust up your crown
beyond the pines
and the Bow River
to where the cold sky
can lay claim to your skree.

I stand below
on the spring-cracked rush
of the Bow
and wonder if the spires
look down at me
with impunity.

The blue ice bonds me
somehow
to your cold spring stone.

TIMBERLINE

If you wish to see
the scope of your existence,
climb to the timberline
of that mountain
and look down.

Tell me now, how big
are your skyscrapers.

WIDE OPEN

Leave it to the wind and the rain
that washes by;
leave it to the sun
and river grass
so that you may know me well.

OF SNOW

A brave swath of yellow grass
sprouts from beneath the burden
of snow
where the hare
cleverly disguised as a ball
of snow
spurts across the meadow
into the trees.

This covering, this frigid mantle
of snow
is surely a hard cloak to bear.

of snow
the river is made
and the warmth of life
assured.

LAST AUTUMN DAYS

Autumn leaves filter down,
stripped from their berths
by the mounting wind.
Later they will fall
of their own accord.

Each windstorm
is the message brought by the wind
to the trees
that winter waits beyond the horizon
where the birds have deserted
to the south
and the grass has resigned itself
to browns and yellows
on bent stalks.

Leigh Clay, circa 1983

Christmas 1985

CREEK

I touch that cake of ice
and it changes direction
in the current,
slipping away from me.

Looking through the shallow depth
of the water
I see a leaf of last autumn
moulded to the shape
of a rock.

I see the tiny grains of sand
skitter across the creekbed.

I see the reflection of my face
cut up and distributed like oil
on the surface of the water
before it is snatched away forever
by the determination
of the current.

HARVEST MOON

The harvest moon
hangs heavy and yellow
over the east slopes
toward Tillicum.

I sit on this hill
beneath its yellow shine
and watch the wind send runnels
through the foot-tall grass
like fingers through hair,
like water over smooth stones.

BULLRUSH

When the phallic cone
of the bullrush
sprays its seed into the wind
its future children are guaranteed.

When I too, touch you
my love,
be assured that our love
will be as guaranteed
as lake wind
at the end of a hot
summer's day.

We delight in the beauty
of the butterfly, but rarely
admit the changes it has
gone through to achieve
that beauty.

Maya Angelou

Marlene Anne Clay married the love of her life, Leigh Everett James Clay, on July 25, 1981 and was widowed in 2012 when Leigh passed away.

Marlene is a retired Social Worker and lives in Calgary, Alberta with Janice, her best friend of 47 years. She is an avid reader, loves live music and says she is addicted to Jon Bon Jovi.

The two books of Leigh's poems that he gifted to her in their first year together is her most prized possession and she is excited to share her gift with you to honour the man whom she loved truly, madly, deeply.

You can follow Marlene on Facebook.com/Marlene Clay or @jonbonrulz on Twitter and Instagram.

CPSIA information can be obtained
at www.ICGtesting.com
Printed in the USA
LVHW070048070422
715583LV00009B/170

9 780228 857921